FIGHT FOR THE FOREST

CHICO MENDES

IN HIS OWN WORDS

The Latin America Bureau

LAB is a small, independent, non-profit-making research organisation established in 1977. LAB is concerned with human rights and related social, political and economic issues in Central and South America and the Caribbean. We carry out research, publish books, and establish support links with Latin American and Caribbean groups. We also brief the media, run a small documentation centre and produce materials for teachers.

FIGHT
FOR THE
FOREST

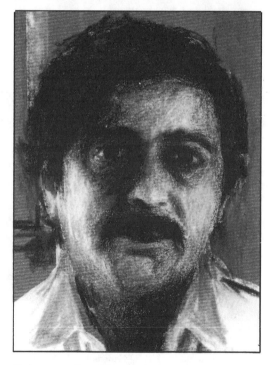

CHICO MENDES
IN HIS OWN WORDS
Additional material by Tony Gross

First published in Great Britain in 1989 by Latin America Bureau (Research and Action) Ltd, 1 Amwell Street, London EC1R 1UL

First printing: August 1989
Second printing: November 1989
Third printing: June 1990
Second edition: May 1992

Fight for the Forest: Chico Mendes in his own words
Adapted from *O Testamento do Homem da Floresta* edited by Cândido Grzybowski, FASE, Rio de Janeiro, 1989
© Latin America Bureau (Research and Action) Ltd, 1989
Translated by Chris Whitehouse
Additional material by Tony Gross
Edited by Duncan Green

British Library Cataloguing in Publication Data
Mendes, Chico
    Fight for the Forest: Chico Mendes in his own words.
    1. Brazil. Rubber industries. Trade - Biographies
    I. Title II. Gross, Tony III. Latin America Bureau
    IV. Testamento do homem da floresta. English
    331.88'1782'0924

ISBN 0 906156 68 8

Drawings by Barboza Leite, taken from *Tipos e Aspectos do Brasil*, Rio de Janeiro, 1975 and Hélio Melo, taken from *O Caucho, a Seringueira e seus Misterios*, Acre, 1986 Historical photographs taken from *Album do Rio Acre*, Pará, Brazil, 1906-07

Cover photo: Marcos Santilli/PANOS
Cover design: Andy Dark, with portrait from photo by
                Camilla Garrett-Jones/OXFAM

Typeset and printed in Canada on environmentally friendly paper.

Trade distribution in UK by Central Books, 99 Wallis Road, London E9 5LN
Distribution in USA by Monthly Review Press, 122 West 27th Street, New York, NY 10001

Contents

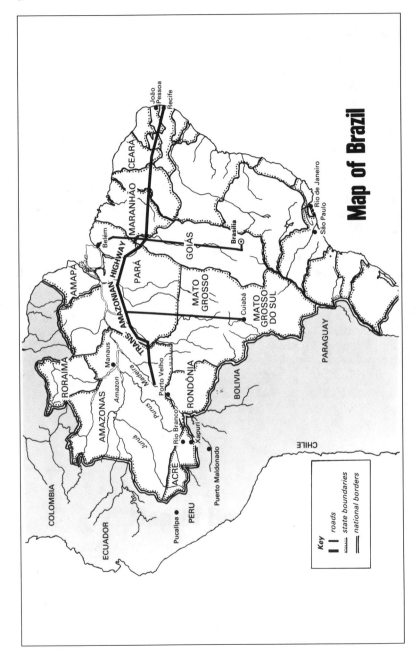

Map of Brazil

Key

- roads
- state boundaries
- national borders

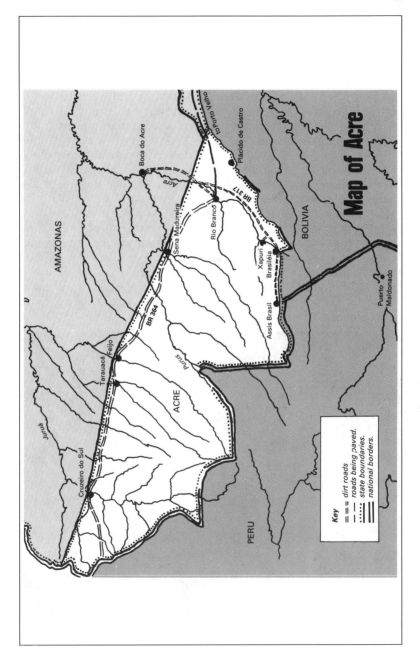

Map of Acre

Key
- = = = dirt roads
- – – – roads being paved.
- ⋯⋯⋯ state boundaries.
- ══ national borders.

AMAZONAS

Boca do Acre

Sena Madureira

Rio Branco

to Porto Velho

Plácido de Castro

BR 317

Xapuri

Brasiléia

BOLIVIA

Assis Brasil

Puerto Maldonado

Feijó

Tarauacá

BR 364

Purus

ACRE

Cruzeiro do Sul

Juruá

PERU

Acre

Biography

Francisco 'Chico' Alves Mendes Filho was born on 15 December 1944, on a rubber estate in Xapuri, Acre, in north-west Brazil. He married Ilzamar G Bezerra Mendes and they had two children. At the time of his death Helenira was four and Sandino was two.

Chico Mendes was President of the Xapuri Rural Workers' Union; member of the National Council of Rubber Tappers; member of the national council of the Trade Union Congress (CUT); an activist in the Workers' Party (PT); and committed to the defence of the Amazonian eco-system.

In 1985, he advised the World Bank and the Inter-American Development Bank on Amazon development projects. In 1987, he received the Global 500 Prize from the United Nations and a medal from the Society for a Better World, New York. In 1988, he was awarded honorary citizenship of Rio de Janeiro.

At 6.45pm on Thursday 22 December, Chico Mendes, trade union leader, rubber tapper and ecologist was assassinated in the doorway of his home in Xapuri, Acre.

Rex Features

Chico Mendes, Ilzamar and Sandino.

STOP!

Stop! That's enough! That cry is in our throats as the new year begins. Enough of death threats and killing for profit and personal gain; destruction and misery; the violence of development projects and ecological holocausts. Enough of the government's abdication of responsibility and connivance with all this death and destruction. Let's all get together and put a stop to it all! Let's build an alternative to all that!

These are my feelings as I write the introduction to this book.

Those who met Chico Mendes will never forget him. He talked softly but was full of energy and won you over through the conviction with which he defended his ideas. He had a forceful but simple, unpretentious personality. This interview with him is a story full of life, work and struggle in the rubber tappers' resistance movement. More than that, it's the story of the struggle to defend the Amazon and, as he used to say, the people of the forest. It is a story about someone who loved life, his community and the place where he lived and worked.

Chico Mendes realised he was carrying out a historic mission as a leader of the rubber tappers' fight to defend the Amazon Forest and establish extractive reserves. He also knew — the struggle taught him — that in defending the rubber tappers' way of life, he was joining hands with many others in the fight to defend an ecological inheritance vital to the peoples of the forest, to Brazilians and to all humanity. Chico's story is about forging a collective response and concrete alternatives to destruction, poverty and oppression in Xapuri.

His shameful assassination on 22 December 1988 by the hired guns of the Acre landowners has transformed his words into a political testament. His death, which he himself foresaw, denounced and fought to avoid, occurred just as he was becoming widely known and recognised as a leader of the rubber tappers and as an ecologist. Chico talked to us and for us. Because of this, all those of us who fight against misery, destruction and oppression were hit by the assassin's bullets. But it was Chico who died. His death will not be without meaning if we preserve his ideas and follow his example.

As a rubber tapper who learned to read and write when he was about twenty years old, he was not a man of letters but a man of words and deeds. In the face of armed violence, he led a movement which used peaceful forms of resistance. In response to deforestation he proposed extractive reserves. To end the semi-slavery of the rubber estates, he fought for the right to work autonomously and collectively. Chico the worker, Chico the ecologist, Chico the pacifist.

He left us a movement. His life and his death transformed his name into a symbol of struggle, faith and hope for a better world, for the peoples of the forest and for all of us.

Cândido Grzybowski, January 1989

The above passage is an extract from the introduction to *O Testamento do Homem da Floresta*, the original pamphlet containing the interview with Chico Mendes.

Introduction

On the morning of Friday, 23 December 1988 I was in Rio, sitting alone at the breakfast table. The front page of the day's *Jornal do Brasil* seemed to have no important domestic stories, so I turned to the inside pages for the first full reports of the PanAm disaster. The phone rang. It was Beto from São Paulo, sounding even terser than usual. 'There's some bad news, have you heard? From Acre.' I felt my pulse quicken, tragic scenarios flashed across my brain. 'No, what's happened?'. 'They've shot Chico, Chico Mendes. Last night.'

So that was it. Of course, I should have guessed. With the shock, anger and resignation came in equal measure. My lack of surprise disturbed me. Had it really been inevitable? We discussed practical things: how to inform those outside Brazil who had known Chico; how people from Rio and São Paulo would be able to get across Brazil to Acre for the funeral on Christmas Eve. I was glad when we rang off.

Folding away the paper I looked again at the front page. This time I saw the headline: 'Trade union leader shot and killed'. I had read it but had failed to see. After all, it was not such an unusual headline. Chico's death was number 90 in 1988's catalogue of murders of Brazilian rural workers and their supporters — church outreach workers, lawyers, education workers.

Chico was President of the Xapuri Rural Workers' Union, based in a small town in the western Amazon state of Acre, near the Bolivian border. He was also the acknowledged leader of Acre's 30,000 rubber tappers. He was 44, married, with two young children: a daughter of four and a son of two. His parents had come from the dry north-east during the Second World War, sent to cut rubber for the allied war effort. Chico was born and brought up in the forest, learning the skills of a *seringueiro*, a rubber tapper. Traditionally rubber tappers were victims of a system of debt bondage, but during the 1960s and 1970s the old system began to collapse in Xapuri. Ranchers from southern Brazil began to buy up rubber estates and clear the forest for pasture. Rubber tappers were evicted, often brutally. Others retreated further into the forest and continued producing on their own account, victims of exploitation by local merchants.

In the early 1970s the Xapuri Rural Workers' Union was founded, and Chico was soon elected its president. A modest and unpretentious man, he was nevertheless a natural leader. As the conflicts over land intensified, the union developed the technique of the *empate*, sometimes translated as 'stalemate' or 'stand-off'. During the dry season ranchers hire labourers to clear the forest for pasture. Just before the rains come in September the cleared areas are fired. Faced with eviction and loss of livelihood, the rubber tappers began to assemble *en masse* at sites about to be cleared, preventing the clearing and persuading the labourers to lay down their chainsaws and go home. Over the last ten years during the months of June, July and August the forests of the upper Acre valley have been the scene of numerous *empates*.

Over the same period others began to realise that not only did this movement represent a fight for social justice, but also a fight against environmental destruction. With the help of a small group of educators and anthropologists, and with modest funding from agencies like Oxfam and Christian Aid, the union began to invest in co-operatives, schools and health posts. Early results showed that once free of debt bondage and economic exploitation the rubber tappers' production was sufficient to permit a substantial increase in their standard of living. In addition, the communities proved they were able to administer their own schools and health posts.

Armed with these arguments the rubber tappers were able to propose a socially equitable and environmentally sustainable development policy for the region based on securing and improving their way of life, rather than official investments in ranching and colonisation projects that would spell disaster both for them and for the forest. Chico played a leading role in negotiating with state and federal governments, with the World Bank and the InterAmerican Development Bank, presenting the rubber tappers' views as a member of the CUT — the Brazilian Trade Union Congress (see chapter 3 footnote 1). He travelled to Europe and to North America. He received two international prizes. At the same time the situation back in Acre was worsening and leaders of the rubber tappers' movement, Chico included, were increasingly at risk.

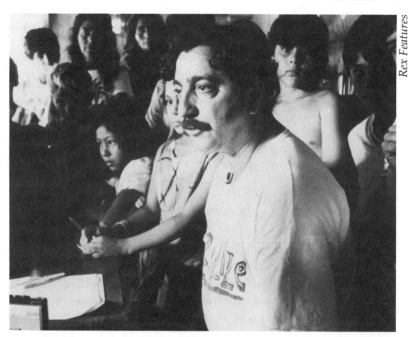

The interview with Chico in this book was part of research commissioned by the Latin America Bureau on social movements in Brazil. The project, under the coordination of Brazilian sociologist Cândido Grzybowski, conducted in-depth interviews with leading figures in these movements. In late November and early December 1988 Chico recorded two and a half hours of interviews in Rio Branco, ranging over the background to his involvement in the rural workers' movement, the growth of the rubber tappers' organisation and the prospects for the future. A few days later Chico was dead.

An explosion of public concern and media attention followed the news of Chico's death. He himself, I am sure, would have expressed amusement and embarrassment at this. He would have been less than amused, I suspect, at the terms in which some of the subsequent debate has been framed in the countries of the North. One of the strands that emerges in this debate is an argument which suggests that since southern governments appear incapable of protecting their fragile environments and, worse, since it now appears the degradation of these environments may provoke global change that will affect us all, the management of such areas ought therefore to be subject to external scrutiny if not control. Behind some environmentally friendly preoccupations lurk politically unfriendly propositions.

To understand the question of tropical deforestation we must look at both the situation in the countries concerned and in our own societies and economies.

It is true that continuation of current rates of tropical deforestation would represent an unprecedented failure on the part of humanity: a failure that would be scientific, aesthetic and, above all, moral. It is true that tropical deforestation makes a triple contribution to global warming: one, because the removal of the trees means they no longer absorb carbon dioxide; two, because burning the forest creates still more carbon dioxide; and three, because the introduction of cattle ranching, as has happened in the Amazon basin, increases the release of methane, another greenhouse gas, into the atmosphere from the unlikely source of bovine flatulence.

Yet only five per cent of the world's emissions of carbon dioxide (which comprises half of the global warming effect) currently occurs in developing countries (excluding China). Around 75 per cent is released from developed countries (North America, Eastern Europe, Western Europe and the Pacific). Western Europe alone is responsible for 15 per cent of the total, three times more than all the developing countries put together. The implications for the North are immense. How can these societies drastically reduce their emissions of greenhouse gases, with all that this implies for the supply and pricing of goods and services, particularly transport and energy? How will the costs be borne? Does the political will exist? Yet until we can demonstrate our commitment and signs of progress on issues such as this, northern preoccupations with southern environmental problems can all too easily be rejected by vested interests in the South as self-serving and hypocritical.

Blaming the victims

Take another aspect of the North-South relationship illustrated by the case of the rubber tappers of the western Amazon. Brazil is the world's most indebted country. It owes over US$120 billion to northern banks and governments. Meeting the payments takes 28 per cent of its export earnings. The international financial system, through the International Monetary Fund, advocates 'adjustment' — reducing imports and maximising export earnings in order to generate the surplus to meet debt obligations. Consequently, countries like Brazil, deprived of new financial support and obliged to cut imports, cannot make the investments needed for sustainable growth. Forced to export as much as possible, as quickly as possible, they turn to boosting the exports of primary products, with all the social and environmental costs that this entails. From the Amazon region minerals, meat, coffee, cocoa, hardwoods, vegetable oils, tropical fruits and a host of other products are sent out onto the world market to raise the foreign exchange to meet the debt payments. The UK is one of the major importers of these products.

Between 1983 and 1987 the Latin American and Caribbean countries paid their creditors US$90 billion more than they received. The UN Secretary General has characterised this as a 'perverse net transfer of resources from developing countries'. Latin American countries owe EC and Swiss banks more than they owe US banks (US$92 billion as against US$80 billion). During this period European banks received a net transfer of almost US$30 billion from Latin American and Caribbean debtors, of which UK banks received a third.

As consumers and bank customers in the North, we benefit from a set of relations that oblige indebted countries to plunder their natural resources. Once again we need to demonstrate a commitment to equitable trading and financial relations between North and South in order to speak from ethically defensible positions on environmental questions in countries like Brazil.

This is not to place the responsibility solely on the North, nor to invalidate the genuine concerns of environmentalists and others for whom the rubber tappers' movement represented hope and for whom Chico's death represented a loss keenly felt. Mutual support and solidarity between communities both North and South seeking to resist and control the forces that dominate them is the key to democracy and sustainable development. In the case of tropical forests, whilst changing production and consumption patterns in the North and advocating equitable North-South relations are clearly necessary, they may not be enough.

Chico was well aware of this. Whilst he sought to construct international alliances, on the basis of mutual understanding and equity, and whilst he wanted to make the European and US public aware of the connections between the struggle he was engaged in and the tinned meat on British supermarket shelves or the hardwood fittings in European bathrooms, he was aware that his struggle lay in Brazil.

A solution to the debt crisis or equitable trading relations would not automatically result in environmental or social improvements in highly indebted countries like Brazil. Substantial political change

At the Second Congress of the National Council of Rubber Tappers and First National Meeting of the Alliance of Forest Peoples.

is also needed. Successive Brazilian governments have had an agenda for the Amazon region in which social justice and environmental protection barely figured. Their aims have included sweetening local elites, generating foreign exchange, fortifying frontiers to forestall or intimidate neighbours and, above all, providing an escape channel for the landless from other parts of the country rather than contemplating agrarian reform.

Forging alliances

It is part of the new demand for democracy and social justice from Brazil's dispossessed and oppressed people that sees the rubber tappers of the western Amazon standing alongside Indians, rural workers, neighbourhood associations, industrial workers and others. They are demanding the right to be involved in taking the decisions that affect their lives, rejecting previous forms of authoritarian political culture, and advocating development policies and priorities that address the basic needs of the mass of the population.

Chico would be the first to admit that he was one amongst many, even in his own community. He was aware of the risks to his life, and had no desire to be a martyr. The purpose of his struggle was after all to enhance life. At the memorial service for him held in Washington in January 1989 one of the readings was from letters he had written shortly before his death:

'My dream is to see this entire forest conserved because we know it can guarantee the future of all the people who live in it. Not only that, I believe that in a few years the Amazon can become an economically viable region not only for us, but for the nation, for all of humanity, and for the whole planet...I don't want flowers at my funeral because I know they would be taken from the forest. I only want my assassination to serve to put an end to the immunity of the gunmen.....If a messenger from heaven came down and guaranteed that my death would help to strengthen the struggle, it could even be worth it. But experience teaches us the opposite. It is not with big funerals and demonstrations of support that we are going to save the Amazon. I want to live.'

I last saw Chico a few weeks before his death. I was in Rio. It was a Sunday afternoon and I was driving to the beach with some friends. As we passed the botanical gardens we saw a march assembling. I saw Chico at its head and thought of stopping to say hello. I hadn't seen him since the beginning of the year, but it was glorious beach weather and I knew that if we stopped we would get into one of those long conversations Chico delighted in and he would end up persuading us to join the demonstration. So we pressed on. I felt guilty, but consoled myself by remembering that I was on my way to Acre and would meet him there. Later we watched the environmentalists march through the centre of town on the television news.

I never did see him in Acre. I was in Rio Branco. He must have been in Xapuri or travelling. Time seemed precious for other reasons and I returned south without seeing him.

Two days after his death, on Christmas Day, I rang a friend in Rio Branco. She told me that one morning the previous week she had arrived late at work and saw Chico driving down the road. He waved at her and shouted something she didn't catch. In her office she was given a message from him explaining that he had waited half the morning to talk to her, but that she shouldn't worry. He would call in next time he was in town. He wished her a happy Christmas.

I suppose all sudden deaths leave this sensation of unfinished business, of conversations hanging in mid-air.

When she saw him he must have been on his way home to Xapuri. Despite the threats he had received, and the advice of his friends, he wanted to spend Christmas with his family. At supper time, as he opened the back door of his modest wooden house to go down to the bottom of the garden for a shower, he was shot in the chest. He staggered into the house and died in the arms of a colleague, his family looking on. The bodyguards provided by the state government disappeared out of the front door, and the police in the town's police station on the next corner did nothing.

Chico did not want to die. The original interview should have served to present the background and demands of the rubber tappers to an outside audience, to reinforce the connections between the preservation of the forest and the need for democracy. It should not have been the chronicle of a death foretold. Nor would Chico have wanted to be cast as a hero: he just wanted people to agree on the need for change and to work together for that change.

Tony Gross
Oxford, June 1989

The history of rubber

The latex from the rubber tree (*hevea brasiliensis*) has been used for centuries by indigenous groups in the Amazon basin for waterproofing bags and footwear. In the 18th century travellers took rubber back to Europe and a flourishing trade grew up as it began to be used in the manufacture of surgical equipment and waterproof clothing. Entrepreneurs from towns on the main Amazon river would make annual expeditions up its tributaries to collect latex and other forest products from Indian communities that had been persuaded or coerced into supplying them.

As demand for rubber grew in Europe and North America in the late 19th century with the advent of the pneumatic tyre and other products, more permanent arrangements evolved. Traders began to bring in non-indigenous labour from outside the region, especially the rural poor fleeing the droughts in north-east Brazil in the 1870s and 1880s. The upper Amazon tributaries (the Madeira, Purus, Jutaí, Juruá, Içá rivers) were occupied and the traditional rubber estate (the *seringal*) created. Conditions were harsh and the indigenous groups were either forcibly incorporated into the labour force of the rubber estate or hunted down.

Nova Floresta, a rubber estate in Acre producing between 15,000 and 20,000 kilos of rubber in 1906.

Xapuri at the turn of the century.

Those that were not exterminated retreated into the forest away from the main rivers.

Great wealth was created. By the turn of the century Manaus had grown from a remote military outpost into the most advanced city in South America with floating docks, electric trams and street lighting, piped water and sewage systems. Much of this investment was British. British banks and commercial firms controlled most of the export of rubber and import of luxury items, and the Booth Line had weekly direct sailings from Liverpool to Belém and Manaus. The great rubber barons of these two cities controlled a network of intermediaries who in turn financed the rubber estate owners (the *seringalistas*). At the bottom of the chain was the mass of rubber tappers (the *seringueiros*), virtual slaves in a system of debt bondage.

In 1876 a British traveller, Henry Wickham, took seedlings of the rubber tree from Brazil to Kew Gardens. By the early years of this century scientists had overcome the problems of artificial propagation and after experimenting in Ceylon, the colonial government encouraged the creation of extensive rubber plantations in Malaya. When these became fully productive after 1910, Amazon rubber exports collapsed, as they could not compete with the far lower prices of Malayan plantation rubber. The rubber estates continued in existence, however, producing for an internal market. When the Allies lost control of Malaya during the Second World War the US government financed the revitalisation of the

Amazon estates and another army of poor north-easterners was drafted into the western Amazon region to tap rubber. These *soldados da borracha* (rubber soldiers) were encouraged to migrate to the region for the duration of the war. The agreement between the US and Brazilian authorities promised them repatriation and military pensions, something that never happened. Chico Mendes' father was a *soldado da borracha*.

In the 1960s and 1970s many *seringalistas* abandoned their estates or sold them to ranchers from other parts of Brazil. This was the case with the region around Xapuri. The 1970s and 1980s have seen a growing conflict between ranchers clearing the forest for pasture, and rubber tappers, in many cases free of the oppressive relations with the *seringalista*, but facing eviction and loss of livelihood at the hands of the rancher.

The life of a rubber tapper

The traditional rubber estate operates on a system of debt bondage. During the rubber boom at the turn of the century the rubber tappers (generally men from the semi-arid north-east escaping the droughts) were obliged to remain single and forbidden to plant food for themselves. They were doubly exploited, obliged to sell their rubber at artificially low prices to the estate and to buy tools and foodstuffs from the estate store. Illiterate and innumerate, they were permanently at the mercy of the *seringalista* and the book-keeper. Leaving the *seringal* was forbidden until the debt was paid off, which rarely happened.

In time, especially after the collapse of the boom, these restrictions were relaxed. Rubber tappers took partners, particularly Indian women, and a new culture evolved, based on this fusion of north-eastern and indigenous characteristics. Although the rubber tapper household began producing some subsistence crops and obtained protein through hunting, pressure to consume from the estate store meant unbalanced nutritional habits with a disproportionate consumption of tinned foods.

A rubber tapper's plan of his trail through the forest, drawn as a tree.

J R Ripper/Imagens da Terra

Children learn to tap rubber from early age.

In many parts of the western Amazon this system remains unchanged, although in the area around Xapuri the *seringalista* has given way to the rancher. This means the rubber tapper, instead of being exploited by the estate owner, is simultaneously exploited by local merchants and facing expulsion at the hands of the rancher.

The rubber tapper household (called a *colocação*) is located in the forest. Each is between 15 minutes to an hour's walk from the next and will have two or more trails (*estradas de seringa*) which pass up to 200 rubber trees as they occur naturally in the forest, before looping back to the rubber tapper's house. The day starts before dawn, when the rubber tapper will set out on a circuit of one of these trails, making a new incision in each tree and leaving a small cup to catch the latex. A second circuit is made to collect the latex. The day ends with the rubber tapper coagulating the liquid latex, either pouring it onto a spit over wood-smoke or adding acetic acid and pressing it into blocks. The trails are tapped on alternate days.

Children learn to tap rubber from an early age. When family labour is lacking, the rubber tapper may employ a youth from outside the family on the basis of a share in the production. Although it is generally the men who do most of the rubber tapping, most women will learn the skills and it is not uncommon for unpartnered women to support their families by tapping rubber.

Rubber tapper's equipment, for collecting the latex
1. scraper
2. knife
3. handle
4. bucket
5. cup
6. bag
7. rubber thong
8. shoulder bucket
9. lamp
10. shotgun
11. strap
12. dagger
13. cartridge case
14. kitbag

Rubber tapper's equipment, for smoking the rubber
1, 2, 4 & 5 adjustable spit for smoking the rubber (3)
  6. large gourd used as basting basin
  7. can for latex
  8. stool
  9. ash pit
10. furnace to burn coconut shells
11. small gourd for scoop

1

First Lessons

My life began just like that of all rubber tappers, as a virtual slave bound to do the bidding of his master. I started work at nine years old, and like my father before me, instead of learning my ABC I learned how to extract latex from a rubber tree. From the last century until 1970, schools were forbidden on any rubber estate in the Amazon. The rubber estate owners wouldn't allow it. First, because if a rubber tapper's children went to school, they would learn to read, write and add up and would discover to what extent they were being exploited. This wasn't in the bosses' interests. Also it was better for production to have the children available for work rather than going to school.

So for many years, the great majority of us could neither read nor write. The rubber tapper worked all year hoping he would finally make a profit but always remained in debt. As he couldn't count, he couldn't tell whether he was being cheated or not.

But something out of the ordinary happened to me. One afternoon in 1962, someone new passed by our house on the rubber estate where we lived. He was a worker, a rubber tapper, but looked and spoke completely differently from the rest. He called by on a day when we had just got back from tapping and were busy curing the latex. He began to chat and the way he spoke intrigued me. He brought newspapers with him. At that time I didn't even know what a newspaper was, but I showed an interest in them and I think he realised I was keen. Anyway, my father and I arranged to go and see him.

One day, we set off to visit his home. To get there, we had to walk for three hours along a narrow trail in the forest. He lived alone in his hut. He said he would like to teach me how to read, and he and my father agreed I could take time off work at the weekends to go and spend some time with him.

Forest politics

Every Saturday I left in the afternoon and walked through the forest for three hours to get to his hut. As we had no text book, he used to use a political column in the newspaper. He received these newspapers a long time after they came out, a month, two months. This went on for several months and in no time I could read and write. My father also understood a little bit and he helped me too, but he didn't have much time to teach me. This other person was much more able, he was very intelligent. I was so interested in what he had to say that at times I spent the whole night awake, listening to him.

After a year had gone by like this, he began to tell me something about himself. One night, he told me had been in the army, that he had been a lieutenant in 1935. He and some of his colleagues had joined the movement led by Luís Carlos Prestes[1] at that time. He told me the country had been in a bad way and that he had decided to fight for the revolution led by Prestes. But Prestes was defeated and many people were arrested. He and other colleagues were imprisoned on the island of Fernando de Noronha.

He had relations on the government side and they managed to arrange his escape by boat from the island to Belém in the state of Pará. There he joined another rebellion and once again he was arrested. He escaped again and went to Bolivia, where in the 1950s he played an active part in the struggles of the Bolivian workers, the miners and the opposition movements. Then there was a great wave of repression and he was one of the people they were looking for, but before they could arrest him he fled into the jungle and made his way through the rubber estates across the border to Brazil.

The Bolivian border was just two hours' walk away from his hut, and he had decided to stay where he was, for safety's sake. So he lived on his own and learned how to tap rubber. He never even learned how to cook. He really did lead a complicated life! After I had known him a year, he told me his name. It was Euclides Fernandes Távora.

The 1964 coup

The most important thing I learned from him was about 1964, when

Wendy Tyndale/Christian Aid

Rubber tapping using a brazil nut pod to collect latex, Xapuri.

The military coup of 1964

The government of João Goulart (1961-64), leader of the Labour Party and bete noire of the armed forces, tried to undertake structural economic and social reforms, provoking intense opposition from conservative forces. The opposition had the support of the US, concerned to prevent radical change in Latin America in the aftermath of the Cuban revolution.

The Goulart years saw increased inflation and the growing organisation of the working class and the dispossessed. Industrial trade unions pressed for reform of restrictive labour legislation, while rural workers' unions were formed for the first time, and the sugar plantations of the north-east witnessed the first attempts to challenge the almost absolute power over life and death held by landowners. Innovative community action and literacy projects began to flourish, under the initiative of the Church or progressive figures like Paulo Freire. Conservative forces, their interests challenged, and the military hierarchy, threatened by growing militancy amongst the ranks, carried out a coup in April 1964 to 'prevent subversion' and 'restore order'.

The military promoted a new economic and social model, attracting foreign capital for a programme of rapid industrialisation by offering political stability and cheap, docile labour. They achieved this through wage control and the concentration of wealth, leading to the coexistence of high growth rates and increasing poverty. Opposition was suppressed by force.

The growing economic crisis, beginning with the oil price rises of the mid-1970s and deepening with the debt crisis after 1982, forced the military to plan its withdrawal from direct political administration, whilst nominating and controlling future civilian presidents. Successive changes in electoral legislation were made to achieve this.

The military's plans went astray when the opposition candidate Tancredo Neves, able to unite a wide spectrum of political forces, won the indirect presidential election in 1985. However he died before taking office and the vice-presidential candidate José Sarney, previously leader of the military's political party and an opponent of democratic reforms, was installed as president. The Sarney government presided over economic mismanagement, growing rural violence and the failure to undertake much-needed measures such as agrarian reform.

The presidential elections in November 1989 were the first direct elections since 1960. In the second round run-off the maverick conservative candidate Fernando Collor de Melo narrowly defeated the PT candidate Luís Inácio da Silva (Lula).

there was a military coup in Brazil. I'd already learned a lot from my conversations with him. He'd managed to get hold of a radio and I learned how to get the Portuguese-language programmes transmitted from abroad. The first programme I used to listen to was transmitted at five o' clock every afternoon by Radio Moscow. Straight after that, there was a programme on the Voice of America and around the same time, a broadcast in Portuguese by the BBC in London. These three programmes had a lot of power in the Amazon.

Every night we discussed the radio programmes. After the coup, for example, we listened to the Voice of America talking about a great victory for democracy in Brazil. Another night, we would listen to Radio Moscow condemning the repression in Brazil and saying the coup was financed by the American CIA and supported by the conservative sectors of the Church. The programme gave a very good analysis. We also learned from these broadcasts that the real patriots of our country were being massacred and many of them had been arrested, tortured, and exiled, while many more had been disappeared or assassinated. They were all activists.

Meanwhile the Voice of America kept on repeating that there had been a great victory for democracy against anarchy, corruption, terrorism and communism and so on. So you see, I learned all the different versions. After every programme, we used to discuss and compare the US and the Soviet versions.

This made me very much more aware in 1965, the last year that I saw much of Euclides. He gave me a lot of advice about how to organise in the trade union movement. He said we had at least 10, 15, 20 years of dictatorship ahead of us but that new unions, new organisations would emerge. Despite the defeats, humiliations and massacres, the roots of the movement were always there, he said. The plants would always germinate again sooner or later, however much they were attacked. He told me nobody had ever been able to eliminate this movement for liberation in the world. It was a very good lesson, a prophecy about our country's future.

Getting involved

Then he said: 'Look, you ought to get involved in trade union organisation in this area. They will emerge, sooner or later, I don't know when, but that is where you ought to be. Don't avoid joining a union just because it is linked to the system, to the Ministry of Labour and the dictatorship.'

'You must get involved', he continued. 'You know, Lenin always said you shouldn't stay out of a union just because it is yellow. You must join it and use it to organise the grassroots, spread your ideas and strengthen the movement. Who knows, you might overthrow that system. The unions may be completely tied to the government but don't worry about their philosophy or about the politics of whoever is in charge. Mind you, they will be servants of the government and you'll need to know about them when you're in there.'

I think that was one of the most important bits of advice he gave me and one of the reasons why I am in this struggle today. Unfortunately, other friends did not have the privilege of knowing Euclides.

In 1968, I tried to organise the rubber tappers and I came up against a lot of problems. I tried to do it on my own — I didn't have any backing. It was during the hardest years of the dictatorship and it was very difficult to get people interested. We had to wait until 1975, at a time when the whole region was under the sway of the landowners, before the first trade unions were formed, on the initiative of CONTAG and according to guidelines drawn up by the Ministry of Labour.

When I heard that the first union was to be founded in Brasiléia, I remembered Euclides' advice and went straight there, without waiting for an invitation. They accepted me and I did a course on trade unionism as part of the union's initial work. I did well. Because of what I had learned ten years previously, I felt at ease taking part in the discussions there, but I soon saw the kind of cautious, conservative thinking that lay behind the union. On the face of it, the union was there to defend the rubber tappers but it was actually all about preserving the status quo. I saw this straight away but it only made me want to penetrate that movement even more.

So I joined the Brasiléia union in 1975. Elias Roseno was elected President, Raimundo Maranhão, Treasurer, and myself as Secretary. Since there was no money to pay any of us, we three took turns staffing the office. I used to stay one, two or three weeks in the union office while the others worked and then we would swap over. Some friends in Xapuri who worked on the rubber estates near to Brasiléia found out I was Secretary and also joined the union, but Xapuri was a separate municipality and I decided to come back and set up a union here.

It was difficult at first, because Xapuri was quite different from Brasiléia. At that time, in Brasiléia, the Church was led by Bishop Dom Giocondo of the prelacy of Acre-Purus. He had come out in

CONTAG and Brazilian unions

Brazil's trade union structure dates from the Estado Nôvo, the period of Getúlio Vargas' dictatorship from 1937-45. Vargas' model was Mussolini's labour code, which states that trade unions are subordinate to the Ministry of Labour. Union membership is obligatory. The Ministry controls the finances, collecting members' dues and apportioning funds within the trade union structure. It can intervene in union affairs, removing officers and appointing its own nominees in certain cases.

Unions are divided up according to category or profession and to their municipality. For example, bank workers in metropolitan São Paulo (composed of various municipalities) will be members of different bank workers' unions depending on where they work. Construction workers in these same municipalities will have their own building workers' unions, as will every other labour category. Each type of union will come together at a state level in a federation, and these federations support a national level confederation.

Under the legislation, contact is prohibited between unions of different labour categories. For example, there is no legal structure whereby bank workers' unions and building workers' unions can meet. (This however has not prevented the de facto emergence in the 1980s of trade union congresses.)

CONTAG (*Confederação dos Trabalhadores na Agricultura*) is the Confederation of Rural Workers' Unions. At the time Chico Mendes is describing, the state of Acre had no rural workers' unions in existence. CONTAG therefore decided in 1975 to send a representative from Brasília to Rio Branco, the state capital of Acre, charged with creating, from the top downwards, rural workers' unions in the municipalities of Acre. The unions in Brasiléia and Xapuri were the first to be formed. By the early 1980s rural workers' unions had been formed in all the municipalities of Acre, together with the state federation of rural workers' unions — FETACRE (*Federação dos Sindicatos dos Trabalhadores Rurais do Acre*).

favour of the rubber tappers, and the inauguration of the union, as well as its courses and training days were all carried out on church premises. Things were different here in Xapuri. In fact, I soon got a police summons for the first time in my life, because a local priest had told the police about my activities. This priest was close to the landowners and against any kind of organisation by the workers. He also happened to be a secret agent of the government's intelligence system, the SNI. His name was Father José Carneiro de Lima.

It was a bit difficult to organise the union here but everyone worked hard to get it going. From 1978 onwards, when I was already in Xapuri, Wilson Pinheiro[2] was elected as leader of the Brasiléia union. He was a very able and courageous person and he strengthened the movement a lot.

Elected by accident

When I was still on the union executive in Brasiléia, but already thinking about moving to Xapuri to help organise a union there, general elections were called. At that time, the military dictatorship allowed only two political parties to function — ARENA, the National Renovating Alliance and the MDB, the Brazilian Democratic Movement. The MDB was generally seen as an opposition party though it was really a party created by the dictatorship. Even so, it was the only party that workers had the least bit of confidence in because it opposed the dictatorship at a very difficult time. There were a lot of people who didn't even feel brave enough to stand as a candidate for an opposition party.

I was invited to stand as candidate for the Xapuri municipal council, because the party needed a minimum number of candidates to be able to take part at all. I accepted just to make up the numbers. When I consulted my colleagues in Brasiléia, they were a bit worried because they didn't think it was the right moment. I felt I should stand because it would help me when it came to organising a union in Xapuri, and in the end people agreed with me.

So I came here to Xapuri and stood as MDB candidate for the municipal council. I was still thinking I was just a name on a list that would allow the MDB to take part nationally. I didn't have any money and I didn't have any experience of party politics. I voted for the opposition and I was opposed to the government, but I didn't fully understand the party political process. In the end, however, I was elected. My lack of experience made things difficult for me. My background was in the trade union movement, but now I had to get on with both the political party and trade union aspects of the struggle.

The party for which I was elected, the MDB, won a total of three seats on the council and the regime's party got four. I knew things wouldn't be easy since the landowners' side had the majority, but I had hoped that at least my two MDB colleagues would show

Forest calendar; each groove marks a day's work.

support for the workers. I was to be disappointed. They didn't share my idea of using the mandate as an instrument of struggle for the rubber tappers. The first initiatives I took on the council were aimed at stopping the expulsion of rubber tappers from their land. This didn't go down very well either with my colleagues or with the majority party. It didn't go down very well either with senior politicians in the MDB and in 1977 I nearly got kicked out of office. I got more and more disillusioned.

I took an active part in founding the union. I wasn't eligible for election to the union executive because I was holding political office but I worked to get colleagues elected. It was from about this time that I began to receive support from the local Church which was going through a process of change after that reactionary priest I mentioned had left.

The years 1978 and 1979 were very difficult for me, what with being a town councillor and involved in the trade union movement at the same time. I was told I couldn't be a member of the union unless I was working in agriculture, so I went out tapping rubber and harvesting brazil nuts while the local council assembly was in recess. After the union allowed me to affiliate, I took part in a lot of its decision making processes.

An injured lion

The situation improved but the political fights with the landowners and the other six town councillors were very rough. It was one of my bitterest experiences but it taught me a lot. It was how I found out about how the party political machine works, how workers are conned. It's a tragic, ridiculous system. Without realising it, workers are like the person who meets an injured lion, cures the lion and then gets eaten by it! The workers strengthen the politicans who then defend the workers' enemies. And many workers have still not discovered this.

At that time I began to get to know a different set of people: the intellectuals, people with an education, students and university professors in other left-wing movements. These people began to try and recruit me and I got involved with another side of things, the clandestine political parties. I even went so far as to participate in the PC do B, an illegal Communist Party at the time. I was attracted by the proposals of the left and began to realise I was in the wrong party, but for tactical reasons I wanted to carry on in the MDB. I felt I ought to continue using the mandate as an instrument of struggle because things would be worse otherwise.

It was towards the end of 1979 that the Workers' Party (PT) was created. Trade unionists in São Paulo and here in Acre asked me to join. It was a difficult decision because the PC do B considered anyone who joined the PT as a traitor. I disagreed with the way the PC do B behaved. We organised together against the landowners but when there was any repression, they disappeared while I had to face the consequences. I kept finding myself on my own. I began to get angry about it and to be suspicious of them, so I left the PC do B and joined the PT.

I became active in the PT. I joined because it was a party that was very attuned to the aspirations of the trade union movement. But I had further bitter experiences, not to do with the national policies of the party but because of various groups that decided to enter it — I was a victim of internal disagreements. In 1982, I stood as a PT candidate for the state legislative assembly but lost. I had to face a lot of internal opposition because the right-wing of the party believed my candidacy would damage the party by leading it to adopt a radical line. The worst people were those linked to the Church, people who were supposed to be progressive. But that's all right, I accepted it as all part of the process of struggle and got on with the job.

I got more and more involved in the trade union movement, feeling it was the best place for me to participate. It all made me remember the advice given to me by Euclides, back in 1965. I continued to be active in the PT but from 1982 onwards I devoted myself to the Xapuri Rural Workers Union.

Today, I am a member of the National Council of Rubber Tappers (CNS).[3] I've kept off the executive to leave space for other members, but I have a leadership role nevertheless. People are saying I should stand for the CNS executive at the next national meeting which is due to take place in March 1989 (see chronology). I believe the CNS can make a very big contribution to the movement, nationally and internationally.

My role, not as a leader, but as a comrade, has been to contribute to the strengthening of our movement, and today I think the CNS has become very important to the struggle. Even though I'm speaking as President of the Xapuri Rural Workers' Union, I think it's the CNS that's the key to strengthening the trade union movement in the Amazon region. As one of its members, I aim to do all I can.

The rise of the Workers' Party

In 1979 the imposed bi-party system of ARENA and the MDB was breaking down and was replaced with new legislation. Although this permitted the creation of new parties, the registration procedures were complex and designed to perpetuate old-style parties under another guise. The PT (*Partido dos Trabalhadores* — Workers' Party) grew out of the metal workers' strikes of São Paulo (1978, 1979 and 1980) together with emerging rural and urban grassroots movements and progressive Church organisations. It represented a new network of community and union organisations which had emerged during the military period and which saw the official opposition party, the MDB, as unrepresentative. They wanted to create a new sort of party, one that was democratic, participative, and built from the bottom upwards.

The founders of the PT managed to stand the new 1979 legislation on its head. The legislation required parties to have local committees in at least 20 per cent of the municipalities in at least 12 states. This was clearly designed to facilitate the registration of previously existing parties, and presumed that no new party would be able to achieve this in the short term. The PT was able to satisfy these draconian requirements within a year by coming into being as the voice of a plethora of already existing groups: union (industrial, rural, professional), neighbourhood, Church and intellectual. By the end of 1981 the PT had over 500,000 members, coming from nowhere to become Brazil's fourth largest party. Unlike other poltical parties, the PT is based on the principles of participation and democratic decision-making, through local groups, regional co-ordination bodies, and state-level committees to the national party conventions.

In electoral terms the PT grew slowly. In the 1982 elections it had a handful of federal deputies and senators elected to the National Congress, but PT President Luís Inácio da Silva (Lula) failed in his bid to be elected governor of São Paulo state. The 1985 municipal elections and 1986 congressional and state elections saw advances for the party, but the major turning point came in the municipal elections of November 1988. With an electorate disillusioned after three years of economic crisis and perceived corruption within the PMDB/PFL alliance supporting President Sarney, many voters turned to the PT. The party increased its overall share of the vote, increased its representation on a number of important municipal administrations and, above all, won the mayoral elections in Porto Alegre and São Paulo, plus the ring of industrial suburbs surrounding São Paulo.

The narrow defeat in the 1989 presidential elections disheartened a party that by the end of the campaign had convinced itself that Lula would be elected. The first two years of the Collor government saw the PT on the defensive and incapable, along with the other opposition parties, of providing effective opposition to Collor.

In the 1990 Congressional elections the PT increased its representation in the Chamber of Deputies and won its first seat in the Senate. In the governorship elections, however, the PT came close to victory in only one state. This was Acre, where the PT candidate Jorge Viana, a FUNTAC forestry engineer running with the support of the CNS and local grassroots organisations, lost to the conservative PDS candidate in the second round run-off.

The presidential election defeat, the party's poor showing in the 1990 governorship elections, the experience of municipal administration in Porto Alegre, São Paulo and Vitoria, plus the strategy re-evaluation induced by the collapse of socialism in Europe, led the November 1991 PT party convention to decide to concentrate on building a progressive left-of-centre bloc with other parties to provide opposition to the Collor government in Congress and to fight the November 1992 municipal elections with joint left candidates.

2

Learning to Fight

With Wilson Pinheiro showing us the way as President of the
Brasiléia trade union, our resistance movement spread across the
region. The years of 1978 and 1979 were especially important in this
process, and the work done at that time made the Brasiléia union
into one of the strongest around. Even CONTAG recognised that.

In 1979, Wilson Pinheiro led a group of 300 rubber tappers to
Boca do Acre, in the state of Amazonas, and drove out a group of
gunmen who were threatening land squatters there. The rubber
tappers only carried knives and sickles, but they still managed to
disarm the gunmen, confiscating more than 20 automatic rifles.
When they got back to Rio Branco they handed the rifles over to the
local army unit, but the local army commander got angry with them
and accused them of wanting to turn the area into another Cuba.
Wilson replied: 'No, we are trying to avoid this place becoming
another Cuba.'

A spiral of violence

This made a big impression on people and got the landowners
worried. As a result, in June 1980, the region's landowners held a
secret meeting about the resistance the rubber tappers were
organising. They decided the solution was to kill Wilson Pinheiro
along with a leader from Xapuri — that could easily have been me.
In this way, they hoped to stop the resistance and carry on clearing
the forest unheeded.

They hired two gunmen for 400,000 Cruzeiros (£3,300) each. On
the night of the 21 July 1980 one of the gunmen went to our office
in Brasiléia and at 7.30 in the evening, right there in the union office,

he shot Wilson Pinheiro dead. The other hired killer went to Xapuri but didn't manage to find any of the people on his list. Luckily, we were all at a union meeting in the Juruá Valley.

The workers were really angry about Wilson's death. We tried to get the police to investigate, setting a time limit of seven days for something to be done. Unfortunately, the law turned a blind eye. We were still in the time of the dictatorship and the only police official who showed any interest in getting to the bottom of the crime was removed from his post by the state's Security Minister.

On the seventh day, the rubber tappers realised the police weren't going to do anything and angrily went off to an estate about 80 kilometres from Brasiléia, where they seized one of the landowners known to have organised Wilson's assassination. It was clear that this particular landowner was part of the whole conspiracy to kill Wilson. The workers gave him a summary trial and condemned him to be shot. He got about 30 or 40 bullets.

The workers were prepared to leave it at that because they thought they had, at least in part, avenged the death of their leader. But this time the police acted fast. In the next 24 hours dozens, hundreds of rubber tappers were arrested, tortured, some of them had their nails torn out with pliers. All because ordinary workers had reacted to a crime committed by wealthy and powerful people.

In a way the movement suffered a defeat in Brasiléia. The repression forced us onto the defensive. But resistance had to go on, though this time with Xapuri as the organisational base. The Xapuri union was founded with a great deal of self-sacrifice in April 1977. The local Church, the middle class and the local authorities put a lot of pressure on us, but despite this, the rubber tappers were very anxious to see things change and to be free from all the pressure and the threats. It all began quite slowly, but the task of organising against the major cases of deforestation got under way again.

In Xapuri we had one particular thing on our minds. We wanted to involve people much more widely in the discussion and preparation of our resistance so that what happened in Brasiléia couldn't happen again. Wilson had centralised things in Brasiléia and when he was killed there was quite a downturn in the resistance. Here in Xapuri we wanted to improve grassroots organisation so the movement would be stronger.

Tony Gross/OXFAM

A literacy class at Floresta rubber estate, a day's walk into the forest from Xapuri. The literacy teacher lives with the rubber tappers for some months and trains further teachers to carry on the work.

Education for a change

From then on, the Xapuri rubber tappers showed the way in the struggle against deforestation. The Xapuri union came up with a proposal to use popular education to help develop our level of organisation, to help make contact with more people and draw them into the movement. People's lack of understanding of their situation had been causing us a lot of problems. The rubber tappers have been here for more than a hundred years with no schools, nothing, while at the same time being brainwashed by the rubber estate owners. People tend to keep that slave mentality and therefore do not involve themselves much in the struggle.

We first began to do some education work in 1979, and from 1982 onwards a popular education programme, based on the concerns and lives of the workers, got properly under way. Things went slowly but even so, the programme began to make a big contribution by getting rubber tappers to think more about what was going on around them. It's something that needs to be a permanent part of our work. There was a literacy programme organised by people linked to Paulo Freire and the Ecumenical Documentation and Information Centre (CEDI). The strengthening of our movement has coincided with the development of the education programme.

Projeto Seringueiro

Projeto Seringueiro (the Rubber Tapper Project) was begun in 1980. In addition to the promotion of co-operatives, the project recognised that the prime need was to increase rubber tappers' self-confidence and understanding, to enable them to administer the co-operatives without the need for outside project workers. For this to happen, those involved needed literacy and numeracy training in order to handle the co-operatives' financial affairs.

From the beginning, the literacy programme, devised by CEDI, was a key part of the project. Potential literacy teachers were chosen by the communities to receive training to improve their literacy skills. They then returned to teach other members of their communities. The initial support came from Oxfam and later from the Ecumenical Services Network (CESE). The federal government, through the National Heritage Foundation of the Ministry of Culture, subsequently supported the project and the state government's education department now provides some of the salaries and running costs. Relations between the rubber tappers and the Project on the one hand and the authorities on the other are often tense.

From the start, the project has worked closely with the rural workers' union in Xapuri.

Projeto Seringueiro is organised by the National Council of Rubber Tappers (CNS) and aims to encourage the rubber tappers to identify more closely with the forest, to understand it, to learn more about it and defend it. It is a slow process, but we are making progress.

At first, the programme was directed only at adults. But the adults began to complain that after a day's work they were too tired to study. They said they were too old and it was more important that the children had the chance to study. They managed to convince the education team, and now the team is putting together material for our children. They learn about our *empates* at school and often insist on taking part themselves!

All this has already been important to our struggle in Xapuri. For example the victory at Cachoeira, the first extractive reserve in Xapuri, resulted from the advances in the level of our organisation, and of course the education work contributed to that.

When we began to try and set up our own schools, we asked international agencies for financial support. We got some help from Oxfam. At that time the landowners were telling the security forces

Cachoeira — success at a price

Cachoeira ('rapids') was the name of the rubber estate in the forest outside Xapuri where Chico Mendes was brought up and started life as a rubber tapper. He worked on the Cachoeira estate from the age of ten until his early thirties, when he began devoting most of his time to the rural workers' union.

In 1987 part of the Cachoeira estate was acquired by Darli Alves da Silva. Using a mixture of inducements and threats, he tried to drive out the 60 families of rubber tappers who had lived and worked on the estate for generations. Chico Mendes invested a great deal of effort and all his powers of persuasion and leadership to convince the rubber tappers of Cachoeira to stay where they were, and Darli issued death threats against him. In the second half of 1988, following the shooting of two youths during the *empate* at the Ecuador rubber estate in May and the assassination of Ivair Higino in June, the federal government sought to defuse the situation by signing expropriation orders for three extractive reserves. One of these was Cachoeira, where the 25,000 hectare estate was allocated to the rubber tappers.

This victory for the rubber tappers was also the death sentence for Chico, as the family of Darli Alves sought to avenge their defeat. The attempts on his life became systematic and on 22 December 1988 he was murdered.

that we were getting money from Moscow to help organise a guerrilla army! This led to an increased presence of the security forces and created a very difficult situation, at least until 1983. But then they realised there was no truth in the landowners accusations and let us get on with our work. We didn't let them intimidate us. In fact, when we saw the security forces getting involved, we realised we must be on the right track!

After that the work went ahead well. We've now got 18 schools in the Xapuri region and we want to use the experience we've gained to help rubber tappers set up schools like ours all across the Amazon region. The education programme is certainly going to make a big contribution to our struggle.

We have now managed to get a grant from CESE to pay the programme's co-ordinating team. In addition, many of the teachers are now getting a salary from the state government, because of the pressure we were able to put on the Education Secretary.

ENCONTRO NACIONAL DE SERINGUEIROS DA AMAZÔNIA

11 a 17 de outubro de 1985
Auditório da Faculdade de Tecnologia - UnB
Brasília - DF

Iniciativa: Sindicato dos Trabalhadores Rurais de Xapuri-Acre. Promoção: Federação dos Trabalhadores na Agricultura do Estado do Acre — Seringueiros do Amazonas — Associação de Seringueiros e Soldados da Borracha de Rondônia. Apoio: Instituto de Estudos Sócio-Econômicos (INESC) — Ministério da Cultura — Fundação Nacional pró-Memória — Universidade de Brasília.

Poster announcing the first national meeting of rubber tappers. The drawing is by Hélio Melo, a rubber tapper.

Last year, we signed an agreement with the Ministry of Education in Brasília for government funds to build our own schools. It wasn't very much money: 1,164,000 Cruzeiros (£16,000) for 12 schools. The work only got done because everybody in the community contributed. The Ministry of Education officials were amazed — when they came to inspect the schools, they said they'd never seen anything like it before. They told us of local authorities that had received a lot more money but hadn't managed to build a third of what we'd done.

There are limits to what the government is prepared to do. It isn't interested in politicising workers, because it knows very well that if workers become politically conscious they learn to stand on their own two feet. But even so, our education work has been positive. We believe that all our advances, the fight against the destruction of the forest, the organising of the co-operative and the strengthening of our union, were all possible thanks to the education programme.

Looking for alternatives

A moment arrived when we began to get worried, because we had got a fight on our hands, the struggle to resist deforestation, but at the same time we didn't really have an alternative project of our own to put forward for the development of the forest. We didn't have strong enough arguments to justify why we wanted to defend the forest.

The CNS grew out of our need to work out alternative development proposals for the Amazon forest. People in the union at Xapuri came up with the idea of organising a national meeting of rubber tappers and forming a commission of rubber tappers to go to Brasília. We decided such a commission should be representative of the whole of the Amazon region.

Mary Allegretti,[1] who worked for INESC in Brasília, thought it was a good idea, and in May 1985 I went to Brasília and had a meeting with officials of the National Heritage department of the Ministry of Culture. I asked for financial support to call a national meeting of rubber tappers, and in the end INESC, National Heritage and other organisations including Oxfam agreed to cover the costs.

This ended up as the First National Rubber Tappers' Congress, held in Brasília. Why Brasília? Because it was the decision-making centre of the country. Also because most of the authorities thought the Amazon region was just one big empty jungle. We wanted to

The Brasília meeting

Over a hundred rubber tappers, representing seventeen rural workers' unions and rubber tappers' organisations from Acre, Amazonas and Rôndonia, travelled to Brasília for the meeting. For most of them this was their first trip outside the region, in some cases the first beyond their immediate home. One woman described how she had travelled to the meeting: two days down the Jutaí river by canoe, two days by river boat down the main Amazon river to Manaus, a day by bus to Porto Velho, meeting up with the rest of the participants for the two day bus ride to Brasília. Prior to this she had never been beyond the mouth of the Jutaí river.

Officials from the Ministries of Industry and Commerce, Education, Health, Agriculture, Agrarian Reform and Culture, together with members of the National Congress also attended. The final document from the meeting listed 63 demands relating to Amazon development policy, agrarian reform, rubber policy, food policy, health, education and culture, pensions and social security. The first two were:

'We demand a development policy for Amazonia that meets the interests of rubber tappers and respects our rights. We do not accept an Amazon development policy that favours large enterprises which exploit and massacre rural workers and destroy nature.'

'We are not opposed to technology, provided that it is at our service and does not ignore our wisdom, our experience, our interests and our rights'.

show them the Amazon was in fact inhabited — there were people living and working in the forest.

The important thing about this meeting was that it would provide an opportunity to set up an organisation, or at least to try and set one up, that would be able to develop alternatives which would justify and strengthen our resistance movement in the fight against deforestation.

The National Rubber Tappers' Congress was to take place in October 1985. After I got back from Brasília, we set up an organising committee composed of representatives of the trade union, the *Projeto Seringueiro* and other organisations. Mary spent her time organising things at the Brasília end. A few comrades were delegated to go and seek out rubber tappers in strategic parts of the Amazon and discuss the meeting.

Finally, in October 1985, we managed to bring together 130 rubber tappers from the whole Amazon region. Observers from the rest of Brazil and from abroad were also present. The discussions at this meeting produced the proposal for extractive reserves in the Amazon. This proposal allowed us to put forward an economic development alternative to back up our fight against deforestation, and the idea really took off. It was from then on that the rubber tappers' struggle began to get known all over the world.

We had meetings with officials of several government departments and agencies where there were some sympathetic officials, and soon the first working group was established to discuss the proposal for extractive reserves in the Amazon. The idea had really caught on.

At the moment, we are preparing for a second national meeting of the CNS which we plan to hold in the second half of March 1989. That meeting will elect an executive which will take over from the provisional executive elected in 1985. So the CNS is now a reality.

The forest world

One reason for the diversity of life in rainforests is their great age. Evolution has rolled on in many rainforests for the past sixty million years, making them the oldest communities on earth.

Another reason for their extraordinary richness and diversity is the hot and moist climate. Because temperatures never drop to freezing point, organisms can grow and reproduce continuously throughout the year. Survival depends not upon enduring periods of extreme cold or drought, but upon finding an ecological niche in which one can hold one's own. The climate provides an abundance of such niches. The transition from aquatic to terrestrial life probably occurred in just such warm, moist conditions. Rainforests are the only places on earth where typically aquatic animals can live out of the water.

One disadvantage of highly specialised species is that, because they depend on a particular set of conditions, they are more likely to become extinct if their environment is disturbed. The US imports more than US$16 million of brazil nuts every year, gathered by Indians and peasant collectors from trees scattered throughout the forest. Some years ago an entrepreneur decided it would be more efficient to grow the nuts on a plantation. The trees were planted, they grew well, and in due course they flowered. But they produced no nuts. No one knows exactly how brazil nuts are pollinated, but it seems to depend on a combination of certain species of bees and orchids which did not exist in the plantation.

Subtract the forest from the ground on which it stands, and with few exceptions you are left with poor soil. Why is it so poor? Partly because it is so old. Soil is a mixture of air, water, decomposed vegetation and broken-down rock. Its fertility depends largely on the quality and age of the rock from which it has formed. The Amazon basin developed between two ancient rock masses, the Brazilian and Guayanan shields, several billion years old. They are amongst the oldest rock formations on earth, and the soil formed from them is ancient, weathered and infertile. Only six per cent of the Amazon basin's soils have no major limitations to agriculture.

The tropical rainforest is a closed system, within which the same nutrients are continually recycled. As soon as a leaf or a branch dies and falls to the ground, it begins to decay. Micro-organisms attack the debris and speed up the process of decay, and specialised roots help the plants absorb the nutrients as soon as they are released.

Because a high proportion of the nutrients comes from above, rainforest trees have many small 'feeding roots' that spread out on the forest floor. Often a thick, spongy mass of roots, fungi, humus, bacteria and other micro-organisms covers the soil. Here in the root mat, which may be as much as 16 inches thick and can be peeled back like newly laid

lawn turf, the forest decomposes and nourishes itself, acting as a slow release fertiliser.

Rainforest canopies cushion the soil from the impact of the rain, protecting it from erosion and landslides. Their roots act as sponges, absorbing the rain and releasing it slowly. This way, the forests to some extent even out seasonal extremes, conducting a steady and moderate flow of rainwater to the world's major rivers. When the forest is removed, so is this moderating influence. During the rainy season the full force of tropical storms is felt at once, and there are no reserves left to ease the hardship of the dry months. With cruel irony, deforestation brings flooding and drought.

Adapted from Catherine Caulfield, *In the Rainforest*, Heinemann, London 1985.

3

Building Bridges

We realised that in order to guarantee the future of the Amazon we had to find a way to preserve the forest while at the same time developing the region's economy.

So what were our thoughts originally? We accepted that the Amazon could not be turned into some kind of sanctuary that nobody could touch. On the other hand, we knew it was important to stop the deforestation that is threatening the Amazon and all human life on the planet. We felt our alternative should involve preserving the forest, but it should also include a plan to develop the economy. So we came up with the idea of extractive reserves.

What do we mean by an extractive reserve? We mean the land is under public ownership but the rubber tappers and other workers that live on that land should have the right to live and work there. I say 'other workers' because there are not only rubber tappers in the forest. In our area, rubber tappers also harvest brazil nuts, but in other parts of the Amazon there are people who earn a living solely from harvesting nuts, while there are others who harvest babaçu and jute.

So what are we really after? Despite the threats, we're fighting for better marketing and price guarantees for rubber. We want better marketing policies and better working conditions for those harvesting nuts. But there are an infinite number of natural resources in the forest, so we also want the government to encourage the industrialisation and marketing of other forest products that it has always ignored in the past.

There are other questions to be considered. A sustainable fishing industry could be developed, exploiting the resource in a rational way. The enormous variety of plants with medicinal properties in this forest could prove very important to the country, if only some

Fruits of the forest

● Brazil nuts (*Bertholletia excelsa*) are produced by the *castanheira* tree, one of the tallest in the Amazon forest. Its branchless trunk rises to a height of 20 metres or more, before forming a wide canopy. The brazil nuts are the seeds (12 to 24) contained in a hard pod (the *ouriço*) somewhat larger than a cricket ball. The pods fall to the ground between December and February and are collected and opened by rubber tappers. The felling of the *castanheira* is prohibited by Brazilian law, but since its germination is dependent upon a complex interaction with the surrounding eco-system, the clearing of the surrounding forest effectively kills it. It is a common sight in deforested areas to see the trunks of the *castanheiras* still standing amid the pasture, sterile monuments to the previous forest cover.

Other Amazon trees and their by-products include:

● Babaçu: either of two large palms (*Orbygnia martiana* and *O. oleifera*) which are highly prized for their usefulness. Oil is extracted from the nuts and used in cooking, as fuel, as a lubricant and in the manufacture of soap. The hard, ivory-like quality of the nuts also means that they can be made into buttons. The husks are used as fuel, the leaves provide a fibre for hat and basket weaving, and the stalks are used in the making of a fermented drink.

● Jute (*Corchorus capsularis*) is a 5 metre high tree brought to the Amazon region from India during the Portuguese colonial administration.

Harvesting jute.

Breaking pods to extract and crush babaçu nuts.

The trunk, when felled and soaked in water, releases fibres used to make sacking and other materials.

● Tucumã (*Astrocaryum tucuma*) is a palm which grows to a height of 15 metres. The leaves, following immersion in water, produce a fibre used for fishing nets, rope and hammocks. The juice of the fruit is a regional drink.

● Patauá (*Oenocarpus bataua*) is another palm growing to a height of 15 metres whose fruit, when boiled, produces an oil used for cooking. The fibres are used for brushes.

● Açai (*Euterpe oleracea*) is a palm whose dark purple fruit produces a nutritionally rich drink which is one of the region's great delicacies.

● Copaiba (*Copeifera langsdorfii*) is also known as the balsam copal tree. Its wood is used for carpentry, while its seed provides a medicinal oil.

● Bacaba is the name given to various palms of the genus *Oenocarpus*, common throughout the Amazon region. The pulp of the fruit provides a drink, the kernels a cooking oil and the palm hearts are eaten.

Commercial potential of the rainforest

Tropical rainforests occupy only seven per cent of the earth's land surface, yet they contain an estimated 40-80 per cent of the world's plant and animal species. Sixty per cent of the remaining tropical forests are in Latin America and of this total over half are in Brazil.

The richness of the tropical forests far exceeds that of other regions of the world:

● The United Kingdom has 1,443 different plant species; Costa Rica, only one fifth the size, has at least 8,000.

● Amazonia contains one in five of all known bird species and at least 2,000 species of fish (ten times as many as in the whole of Europe).

● At least a quarter of all pharmaceutical products are derived from tropical forest products, despite the fact that only one per cent of all Amazon plants have been intensively examined for their medicinal properties. Tropical forest plants have so far provided treatments for leukaemia; Hodgkin's disease; breast, cervical and testicular cancer, as well as a host of analgesics, antibiotics, heart drugs, enzymes, hormones, diuretics, anti-parasite compounds, ulcer treatments, dentifrices, laxatives, dysentery treatments and anti-coagulants.

● Of the 90,000 plant species in Latin America only 10,000 have been tested for anti-cancer properties. Scientists expect that at least ten per cent of the untested plants will reveal some form of anti-cancer activity. A species of alexa tree, found in the northern Amazon basin and Madagascar, contains the plant alkaloid castanospermine which is being investigated at St Mary's Hospital in London as a possible treatment for some forms of AIDS.

research was done. The universities, not only in Acre, but throughout Brazil, should spend time researching the Amazon region. I believe if this happened, and if the government took it all seriously, then in ten years the Amazon region could be very rich and have an important role in the national economy.

Where did we get the idea of setting up the CNS? We discovered there is something called the National Rubber Council which represents the interests of landowners and businessmen but not the interests of the rubber tappers, so we thought, why not create an organisation as a counterweight to all that bureaucracy and try to stop the government messing the rubber tappers about? The First National Congress set up the CNS and elected a provisional executive committee.

The CNS is not meant to be a kind of parallel trade union, replacing the Xapuri Rural Workers' Union, for example. It is just an organisation for rubber tappers. The growth of the trade unions was very important for us, but other agricultural workers including day labourers and so on are also members of the same union. Other kinds of agricultural workers have been seen as having particular needs and interests, but not rubber tappers; it's as though we were something that existed only in the past. So one of the reasons for creating the CNS was to recognise the rubber tappers as a particular group of workers fighting for a very important objective — the defence of the Amazon forest. The idea went down very well.

The Indians

We also wanted to seek out the leaders of the Indian peoples in Acre and discuss how to unite our resistance movements, especially since Indians and rubber tappers have been at odds with each other for centuries. In Acre the leaders of the rubber tappers and Indian peoples met and concluded that neither of us was to blame for this. The real culprits were the rubber estate owners, the bankers and all the other powerful interest groups that had exploited us both.

People understood this very quickly, and from the beginning of 1986 the alliance of the peoples of the forest got stronger and stronger. Our links with the Indians have grown even further this year. For example, a meeting of the Tarauacá rubber tappers was attended by 200 Indians and six of them were elected to the Tarauacá Rubber Tappers' Commission. Indians are now beginning to participate in the CNS organising commissions. In Cruzeiro do Sul

Indian children playing on the river, Rondônia.

about 200 Indians are active in the movement and this year they have even joined in our *empates*.

Our proposals are now not just ours alone, they are put forward together by Indians and rubber tappers. Our fight is the fight of all the peoples of the forest.

When the Minister of Agriculture met a joint commission of Indians and rubber tappers in his office, he was really taken aback. 'What's going on?', he said, 'Indians and rubber tappers have been fighting each other since the last century! Why is it that today you come here together?'

We told him things had changed and this meant the fight to defend the Amazon was stronger. People really took notice of that.

Spreading the resistance

Our resistance began in Xapuri, where rubber tappers were in the forefront of the movement. But now our aim is to spread the resistance movement right across the whole Amazon region. Rubber tappers from Brasiléia, from all over the states of Acre, Rôndonia,

Acre's Indians

Reliable 1987 estimates give an indigenous population of 6,600 in Acre and south-western Amazonas in at least 42 separate locations. None of these areas has undergone the whole process of registration by the Brazilian government, a right theoretically accorded the communities by the Brazilian constitution. Recently the government has announced its intention to drastically reduce the size of the areas the communities are entitled to. The population is composed of 15 different indigenous groups: Apurinã, Arara, Iauanauá, Jaminawa, Kampa, Katukina, Kamanawa, Kaxarari, Kaxinaua, Kulina, Machineri, Masko, Nuquini, Papavo, and Poyanawa. The total indigenous population of Brazil is estimated at around 200,000.

With the exception of one or two still uncontacted groups, all of these communities have been in contact with non-indigenous society. The advance of rubber tapping activities into the upper rivers of Acre and south-western Amazonas from the 1870s led either to Indian communities being incorporated into the rubber economy or to their retreating ever further upstream. Many rubber estates organised hunting expeditions (*correrias*) to locate indigenous groups and either massacre them or bring them in to the *seringal*. These expeditions took place until after the Second World War and rubber tappers were forced to take part by their employers. The current alliance between rubber tappers and Indians in Acre is all the more striking given the previous history of antagonism between them.

The region's indigenous communities practise a mixture of subsistence agriculture, hunting and fishing, and collecting forest products — above all rubber and brazil nuts. Although previously some groups lived in substantial communal longhouses (*malocas*), a normal village now consists of a collection of houses built in the regional style (wood or split palm, with a wooden or thatched roof and raised on stilts), surrounded by a cleared area for domestic animals and with nearby gardens. If the village is not on the river bank, there will be other water sources for drinking and washing nearby. All the communities come under the administration of the federal government's National Indian Foundation (FUNAI), and some will have a FUNAI post installed in the village. Many communities are also the object of missionary activity: Catholic and Protestant, Brazilian and foreign.

In recent years the indigenous communities of the region have made considerable progress in overcoming the prevailing racism and establishing their right to participate in local affairs. This progress has been achieved despite opposition from FUNAI and local politicians. The communities have been helped in this process of revitalisation by the local branch of UNI (the Union of Indigenous Nations) and the

Tony Gross/OXFAM

As with the rubber tappers, Indian families clear only a small area around their houses.

Pro-Indian Commission of Acre, a group of anthropologists, teachers and others working with the communities on education, health, economic and consciousness-raising projects.

Amazonas, Amapá and representatives from the only remaining rubber tappers in Pará all came to the First National Congress.

We were particularly keen to get the rubber tappers of Brasiléia and Assis Brasil organised because of the plans to pave the BR 364 road and build a road link to the Pacific. Also because of the BR 317. We knew the paving of these roads would lead to more and more land speculation, and the greed of the landowners would make them grab the land near the roads. We then turned our attention to organising in the Juruá valley, where rubber tappers worked in conditions of near slavery.

We are anxious to organise in Rôndonia because of the extent to which the forest is being destroyed there. There is also a lot of grassroots work being done on the banks of those far-away rivers of the state of Amazonas. But, at the beginning, it was in the Acre valley that the movement grew most quickly.

Chico Mendes on the BR 364 road between Rio Branco, Acre, and Porto Velho, Rondônia.

Looking for allies

Our biggest assets are the international environment lobby and the international press. I'm afraid we have had more support from abroad than from people in Brazil, and the opposite should be the case. It was only after international recognition and pressure that we started to get support from the rest of Brazil.

Links between our movement and other workers' organisations are quite weak in general. We do have good links with organisations that have only emerged recently, like our own, for example the Landless Workers' Movement (*Movimento dos Trabalhadores Sem Terra*). We've got strong links with the CUT trade union federation and their third national congress (in 1988), unanimously adopted a motion put forward by the Xapuri trade union, calling for the defence of the Amazon region by the peoples of the forest.

We haven't had a very good relationship with the National Agricultural Workers' Confederation (CONTAG). They haven't given us much support, but they respect us a lot, despite us being affiliated to the CUT rather than the CGT.[1]

We want to get on well with all the country's labour organisations. We would be quite happy to get support from

Roads to ruin

Environmental destruction in Amazonia follows the roads. As soon as all-weather routes are completed, an influx of poor landless farmers and wealthy cattle ranchers begins to hack down the forest to set up farms on soil which often proves barren once the forest cover is removed. Seen from the air, the main highways and smaller feeder roads are bordered by a roughly 12 mile area of destruction on either side. Beyond 12 miles, the forest cover is usually intact.

Long distance road construction in the Amazon dates from the 1960s. Along with the Transamazônica and the Belém-Brasília highways, the BR 364 Cuiabá to Porto Velho highway was started at this time. From Porto Velho it continued to Rio Branco, crossing Acre to Cruzeiro do Sul. At the same period the BR 317 was begun, from Rio Branco northwards to Boca do Acre, and south to Xapuri, Brasiléia and Assis Brasil. However they were not paved and therefore impassable for most of the year, so their impact was only local.

In the late 1970s Brazil sought World Bank funding to pave the BR 364 from Cuiabá to Porto Velho and to colonise the central part of Rôndonia on either side of the road. This was the North-West Brazil Integrated Development Programme or *Projeto Polonoroeste*. The social and environmental consequences of this in a region which had hitherto been virgin rainforest populated by Indians and rubber tappers are discussed below.

By 1985 the Brazilian Government, wishing to pave the Porto Velho to Rio Branco stretch, was negotiating another loan, this time with the Inter-American Development Bank. Aware of the criticisms of the *Polonoroeste* project, the Bank tried to write in measures to protect the environment and the local Indian communities. Although by the time of Chico Mendes' death disbursal of the loan had been halted, the paving of the road is being undertaken with domestic capital.

There are plans to extend the paved road network further westwards into Peru. In the early 1980s the state government of Acre discussed with Peru the upgrading of the BR 317 to the Peruvian border, where it would link with a road to Puerto Maldonado and the Pacific. Recent planning appears to favour the paving of the BR 364 to Cruzeiro do Sul, which would continue to the Peruvian city of Pucallpa.

One of the main interested parties in a Pacific outlet, apart from Brazilian exporters to Pacific markets, is Japan. The world's biggest importer of raw materials, Japan has identified Brazil as a major long-term supplier of minerals, timber and grains. These are produced either in the Amazon basin or in the Brazilian mid-west. For Japan the

Tony Gross/OXFAM

Preparations for paving the Porto Velho-Rio Branco stretch.

Pacific route makes commercial sense, although it could lead to vast new areas of Amazonia being devastated. The Japanese are reported as having offered to finance the Pacific link from Acre westwards, although they denied this in early 1989.

anybody in the CGT, because we just want to make our movement stronger. We welcome any support, any alliance, as long as the people concerned are committed to our struggle.

Political parties

If the CNS is to become stronger, it must avoid identifying itself too closely with any one political party. That is my position and I have defended it at seminars and meetings in Rio de Janeiro, São Paulo and the US.

So far, the PT is the only party to select rubber tappers as candidates for political office. Despite all its problems, the PT has been the only party that has given us significant support. I've often

Tony Gross/OXFAM

The road from Rio Branco to Xapuri.

felt we could build stronger links with parties other than the PT; left-wing parties with a history of struggle. Unfortunately, we have to live with the sectarianism that is a feature of our country's politics.

In Rio de Janeiro, for example, when I was asked to help launch a group in support of the peoples of the forest, I was advised by some left-wing colleagues to avoid getting caught in the cross-fire between the other parties. When I arrived, the PT and the PV (Green Party) were fighting over who I 'belonged' to. I kept well clear of all this and ended up contributing to a seminar at the ABI where there were the PV, PT, PSB and PCB and other independents, everybody together in support of the proposed support group.

The Church

We have had a lot to do with the Church but there have been clashes at times, because although the Church has an important role in our struggle, it is only prepared to go so far. For example it has been very difficult about our interest in linking up with political parties. The political space the Church has given us has been very important

The Church

Brazil has the largest Catholic congregation in the world and no other country has as many priests, nuns and bishops. The progressive wing of the Brazilian Catholic Church was active in social movements before the 1964 coup, and during the military regime the Church was the only force able to work openly on behalf of the poor and the oppressed. Relations between Church and state have often been strained, leading Helder Camara, one of the most prominent Church opponents of the military regime and formerly archbishop of Olinda and Recife, to remark, 'Why is it that when I give help to the poor they call me a saint, but when I ask why they are poor in the first place, they call me a communist?' Many members of the churches, lay and ordained, have suffered for their support of grassroots movements.

Throughout the 1970s and 1980s the Catholic Church, as part of its 'option for the poor', set up thousands of grassroots 'christian base communities' promoting religious teaching and social action. Congregations were taught that not only were present social and political structures not the will of God, but that a radical change in society could correspond much more closely to Christian values and aspirations.

In addition to creating local Christian base communities, the Church set up various national-level pastoral organisations. Two that were represented in Acre at this period were CIMI, the Indigenous Missionary Council, and the CPT, the Pastoral Land Commission. They served to offer support, spiritual and political, to Indian and peasant communities respectively.

Acre contains two dioceses: Acre-Purus in the east and Juruá in the west. The diocese of Acre-Purus is administered by an Italian order and the bishop is a prominent figure in the progressive wing of the Church, having been president of the CPT. The diocese of Juruá, based in Cruzeiro do Sul, is administered by a German order.

With the arrival in the western Amazon of poor colonists from southern Brazil, in many cases descendants of 19th century German immigrants, the Brazilian Lutheran Church also has progressive pastors and lay workers helping grassroots causes, including rubber tappers and Indians, in Acre.

Tony Gross/OXFAM

Evangelical missionaries in Rondônia.

and recently things have improved, for example the Pastoral Land Commission (CPT) has been more actively involved in our movement after a period in which it vacillated in its attitude towards us. We have good links with the Prelacy of Acre-Purus, but things are much worse in the Juruá Valley where the Church is very conservative. We have a good relationship with the Church at Carauari, another region in the state of Amazonas. I think the links we've had with the Church have been positive and we've been able to build up a working relationship which benefits both the Church and the rubber tappers. The Church cannot give up on us now, after having worked so hard with us in the 1970s.

Cities and students
People in the cities have always ignored us. However, since the CNS was set up we have begun to get some support, for example from Acre University, which is quite an important political institution. We know the great majority of professors in the university either support the UDR or are very conservative, but we hope to get some support from the new Rector there. Student

support has been a bit unsteady but it's increasing now the Greens are getting organised in Acre.

We have found it very difficult to get proper legal assistance. The Acre Federation of Rural Workers' Unions (FETACRE), which ought to support us, has refused us assistance. Their lawyer is more interested in taking on cases for individual small landowners who are able to pay him a bit. We prefer not to have anything to do with him.

Our union doesn't have enough money to employ a lawyer, but in July 1988 the Institute of Amazon Studies helped us obtain the services of a lawyer from Paraná, Genésio Felipe. He gives legal advice to the rubber tappers through the CNS, the individual unions and the Acre Pastoral Land Commission. He covers the whole of Acre, so he's got a big job on!

I'm afraid we don't get much help from the lawyers round here. There are dozens of lawyers in Acre but they are all the children of landowners and other sectors of society that are against the workers' movement.

4

The Landowners Strike Back

We know we face powerful opposition. As well as the landowners and businessmen who dominate the Amazon region, we are up against the power of those who voted against land reform in the Constituent Assembly. The voting power of these people in Congress has been a problem for us and has encouraged the growth of the right-wing landowners' movement, the Rural Democratic Union (UDR). The defeat of the land reform proposal was a big victory for the landowners and land speculators. Now, since the establishment of the UDR in Acre, we've got a real fight on our hands. However, we also believe our movement has never been stronger.

You can already see how strong the UDR is in Acre — it's just organised its first cattle auction to raise funds. We know, through people who have been to UDR meetings here, that their aim is to destroy the Xapuri union by striking at the grassroots organisations of the Xapuri rubber tappers. They think if they can defeat Xapuri they can impose their terms on the whole state and further afield in the Amazon region as well. The Governor of Acre himself told me this. Just to give you an idea, it was after the UDR's official launch here in Acre that the first drops of blood were spilt in Xapuri.

You might not believe it but among our allies at the moment are the rubber processing plant owners. They are not people we can trust very far — for a start, they are also timber merchants. But because they profit from exporting rubber, they are now making overtures to the CNS. They say we should fight together against the abolition of the Rubber Development Board (SUDHEVEA).[1] This is quite a complicated situation because on the one hand we have to defend the interests of the rubber tappers, but on the other we know

Land, power and the UDR

For most of its history, land and power have been synonymous in Brazil. Political power, locally and nationally, lay in the hands of large landowners who traditionally exercised powers of life, and often death, over the mass of the rural population. The modernisation of Brazil after the Second World War saw the beginnings of a movement for agrarian reform; the dismantling of enormous landed estates (often unused for agricultural purposes) and redistribution of land to small farmers in the interests of social justice and increased productivity. It was fear of the growing impetus for agrarian reform that lay behind the 1964 coup.

During the period of military rule, land concentration increased, as did the number of landless families forced to migrate in search of land and work.

The civilian government that took office in 1985 initially said it was committed to massive agrarian reform. It created an Agrarian Reform Ministry and in May 1985 published the draft agrarian reform plan. Started from the concept of social justice, the plan proposed the redistribution of 43 million hectares (168,000 square miles — an area three times the size of England) in five years. The proposals were welcomed by rural workers, but condemned by landowning interests. Over the next six months the government was intensively lobbied by landowners and when the revised plan became law in October 1985 its basic thrust had been altered to a preoccupation with productivity rather than justice. This time it was the landowners who welcomed it, while it was condemned by rural workers.

The rival groups lobbied the National Constituent Assembly when it met in 1987 and 1988 to draft a new constitution, and the landowning interests won. The sections of the constitution which refer to agrarian reform are now more conservative and restrictive in their application than the previous legislation of 1964. A large part of the conservatives' success was due to the UDR, the landowners' organisation that successfully oiled the wheels of the Constituent Assembly whilst at the same time intimidating rural workers and their allies.

The UDR (União Democrática Ruralista — Rural Democratic Union) came into being in 1985 following the publication of the first national agrarian reform programme. Its founder was a rancher and doctor from the mid-western state of Goias, Ronaldo Caiado. The UDR grew quickly, initially through the ranching and agro-industrial regions of the mid-west and São Paulo, but soon forming local groups throughout Brazil, including Amazonia.

In addition to relying on the personal wealth of many of its members, the UDR raises funds through the auction of donated cattle at large public rallies. During the debates on agrarian reform in the constituent assembly in 1987 and 1988 the power of the UDR's organisation became apparent. In addition to intense lobbying in the assembly, and packing the public galleries to intimidate the advocates of agrarian reform, the UDR organised mass rallies in Brasília. On one such day Brasília's airport ran out of parking space for the hundreds of private planes belonging to UDR supporters.

The UDR claims that it controls a substantial block of members of the National Congress, and voting patterns in the Constituent Assembly confirm this. It also claims that many of the mayors elected in the November 1988 elections, particularly in the richer rural areas of southern and mid-western Brazil, are UDR sympathisers.

Although the UDR has consistently denied having paramilitary forces, the levels of rural violence have grown steadily over recent years and many of the hired guns implicated in the assassination of rural workers and their supporters have been linked to UDR supporters.

During the Sarney government less than three per cent of the 1985 agrarian reform programme was carried out. The Agrarian Reform Ministry (MIRAD) had five different ministers over this period and was notoriously inefficient.

When the Collor government took office MIRAD was abolished and its responsibilities transferred to the Ministry of Agriculture. With a representative of São Paulo agribusiness as minister, one of the political successes of the Collor government has been to demobilise the pressures for agrarian reform and lower the visibility of the issue on the political agenda.

the abolition of SUDHEVEA poses a threat to rubber marketing and export.

Whatever the rights and wrongs of the matter and though it has got a lot wrong with it, SUDHEVEA's attempts to improve the rubber marketing structure in the Amazon mean that it's something worth defending in today's circumstances. This is the basis on which the processing plant owners are proposing a tactical alliance with us.

However, generally speaking, the landowners and businessmen of Acre, and the whole region for that matter, are organising resistance to our demands. In this fight, our only defence is the pressure put on the authorities by Brazilian society and the international scientific community.

The government takes sides

There was a time when the state government seemed to be paying

Neil MacDonald/OXFAM

Rubber tappers occupying the Xapuri IBDF office are evicted by local military police.

a lot of attention to environmental problems and to the rubber tappers.[2] But we soon realised it was just putting on a show of defending the environment so the international banks and other international organisations would approve its development projects.

We can't see how the authorities can say they defend the ecological system while at the same time deploying police to protect those who are destroying the forest. That happened, for example, in the case of the Ecuador rubber estate where there were many nut and rubber trees. The Governor was warned several times about what was going on there. In fact, I personally warned him and suggested he go and look at what was happening for himself. I told him he was being very hasty in sending police there. Fifty hectares of virgin forest were cut down, but thanks to the pressure, thanks to the hundreds of telegrams sent to the Governor by national and international organisations, we managed to get him to withdraw the police from the area and so saved about 300 hectares of forest.

In the area they destroyed there, the last harvest produced 1,400 cans of brazil nuts,[3] a good crop. We challenged the owner of the land and the Governor himself to work out the annual income per hectare produced by forest products such as brazil nuts and rubber

Victory at Ecuador

In May 1988 the federal forestry board (IBDF) granted permission for the Delta construction company, which had recently acquired the Ecuador rubber estate in Xapuri, to clear 50 hectares of forest for pasture. The Rural Workers' Union of Xapuri and the CNS objected that the licence was illegally granted and that Delta was actually planning to clear 300 hectares.

With no response from IBDF, the rubber tappers staged an *empate* at the scene but were dislodged by police. They then occupied the IBDF offices in Xapuri, asking the state government in Rio Branco and the IBDF headquarters in Brasília to revoke the licence.

On the night of 24 May 1988, two gunmen on a motorbike fired shots at rubber tappers sleeping on the porch of the occupied IBDF offices. Two youths were hit and required emergency treatment. The bike was reliably identified as belonging to one of the sons of Darli Alves da Silva, responsible six months later for the murder of Chico Mendes.

Following protests by the rubber tappers, supported by demonstrations by the Green Party in Rio de Janeiro, extensive press coverage and telegrams from abroad, the government finally revoked Delta's permission to clear the area.

and then compare it with that produced by grazing cattle there. They refused because they knew we could prove the income from one hectare of forest is 20 times greater than when the forest is cleared and given over to cattle.

We quoted decree law 7.511 of 30 July 1986 and regulation 486 of 28 October 1986 which prohibit the cutting down and sale of brazil nut and rubber trees and the deforestation of hillsides. There were two hillsides in the area being cut down on the Ecuador rubber estate and the law was completely flouted. After the second *empate*, when the rubber tappers managed to stop work going ahead, the local IBDF representative appeared and without even inspecting what was going on, told the landowner he could go ahead and clear the forest. He gave the landowner a licence even though the landowner did not present, as he should have done, a written plan for managing the area.

Another law — I can't remember its number — says you can only clear up to 50 hectares of forest without presenting a forestry management plan. Further on it adds that it's forbidden to cut down any area of forest on hillsides or where there is a concentration

Chico Mendes speaks to 150 rubber tappers in the church on the day after the shooting.

of brazil nut and rubber trees. None of these laws were respected. The Governor himself didn't even consider them and the IBDF certainly didn't.

We do have a good relationship with the Acre Technology Foundation (FUNTAC) which is a state government agency.[4] They really understand how difficult the lives of rubber tappers are and recognise that deforestation is a problem. But despite the good relationship we've got with FUNTAC, we have no confidence left in the state government. How can we believe a Governor who says he defends the forest, and visits Rio and Japan to talk about defending the forest, but who then orders the police to go and protect the people who are destroying it? He ought to be using the political power that his office gives him. If he used his power in favour of the workers he'd certainly get their support.

Holding back progress

People have used all kind of arguments against us. The landowners say we're holding back progress and harming the country's economy. They say rubber is not important to the economy and the future lies with cattle raising. Others say the Amazon is a vast expanse of uninhabited territory and that it should be developed. All kinds of reactionary arguments are used against us. Our enemies work hard at putting forward their arguments to try and undermine our own. However, the national press has now started to realise that the defence of the Amazon is really an issue.

But anyway, we can deal with the arguments that are used against us. To those who say Acre should be producing food, we say there is plenty of land for that. What are the big colonisation projects supposed to be producing? Anyway, all it needs is for the government to develop an agricultural policy that takes into consideration the region's small farmers. There should be no problem about growing enough food.

The rubber tappers aren't saying that nobody should lay a finger on the Amazon. No. We've got our own proposals for organising production. The rubber tappers and the Indians have always grown their subsistence crops but they've never threatened the existence of the forest. It's the deforestation carried out by the big landowners to open up pasture for their cattle that is threatening the forest. Often, these people are just speculating with the land. What happens in Xapuri and other parts of the Amazon is that these people cut

Tony Gross/OXFAM

A brazil nut tree stands alone after the rest of the forest has been cleared.

The road to Rôndonia

Large-scale organised colonisation schemes in the Amazon region began in the 1970s. When the government built the Transamazônica highway, it included an ambitious colonisation programme as an attempt to settle landless peasants from north-east Brazil and defuse demands for agrarian reform. Both the highway and the colonisation were failures, although sizeable numbers of poor colonists were settled in the Altamira region. Private colonisation schemes were set up in northern Mato Grosso, mostly involving migrants from southern Brazil who had lost their lands as a result of the boom in soya production.

With the beginning of the *Polonoroeste* project in Rôndonia, vast numbers of people from both southern Brazil and the north-east flocked to the area, looking for places on official colonisation projects or seeking to settle spontaneously wherever land was available. At one time over 7,000 families a week were moving along the BR 364 highway. Without a proper land register or the administrative capacity to control this influx of people, the authorities could do little to avoid the chaos that followed.

Such credit and extension services as existed were directed towards ranching and the promotion of high-value export crops such as coffee and cocoa. Adverse circumstances, including the poor quality of most of the soils and total unfamiliarity with a tropical forest environment, plus extremely high malaria levels, led to tragic failure for many of the colonists.

Following severe criticism the World Bank has acknowledged that the *Polonoroeste* project was ill-conceived and poorly administered. The fear of the rubber tappers and Indians of Acre has been that the paving of the road into Rio Branco will trigger a similar wave of uncontrolled migration, with the same disastrous social and environmental consequences.

Although there are ways of settling more people and increasing food production in tropical forest areas without this level of destruction, it is important to recognise that the pressure on land in the Amazon region is the result of the failure to carry out agrarian reform in other regions of Brazil, where land concentration, and therefore the numbers of landless rural families, is currently increasing.

down 10,000 hectares, turn half of it into pasture for their cattle and let the other half grow wild. They are really just involved in land speculation.

The landowners use all the economic power at their disposal. They bribe the authorities; it's common knowledge that they've bought off the IBDF staff in the Amazon region. They also use the

Tony Gross/OXFAM

Road clearance and settlement can cause a 12 mile corridor of devastation. A township in Rondônia — similar settlements could start in Acre.

law. They request police protection for the workers hired to cut down the trees, saying it is their land so they can do whatever they like with it. They accuse the rubber tappers of trespassing when we try and stop the deforestation. They turn to the courts for support and protection, claiming the land is private property. But the rubber tappers have been here for centuries!

There has been less pressure from the police in the last two years because we are able to present reasoned arguments to them. When we organise an *empate*, the main argument we use is that the law is being flouted by the landowners and our *empate* is only trying to make sure the law is respected.

The other tactic the landowners use, and it's a very effective one, is to use hired guns to intimidate us. Our movement's leaders, not just myself but quite a few others as well, have been threatened a lot this year. We are all on the death list of the UDR's assassination squads. Here in Xapuri, these squads are led by Darli and Alvarino Alves da Silva, owners of the Paraná and other ranches round here. They lead a gang of about 30 gunmen — I say 30 because we've counted them as they patrol the town. Things have changed recently because we managed to get an arrest warrant issued in Umuarama, in the state of Paraná, for the two of them. I don't know whether it

Tony Gross/OXFAM

Cleared land can support cattle — for a while.

was the federal police, but somebody tipped them off. Now they're both in hiding and have said they'll only give themselves up when I'm dead (see epilogue).

We are sure this will be the landowners' main tactic from now on. They are going to fight our movement with violence and intimidation. There's no doubt in our minds about that. The level of violence that has been common in the south of the state of Pará is already spreading to Xapuri, to Acre.

Rich men's law

The law has always been on the side of the rich. One of our problems is how to cope with this bias in the judicial system. We often turn to it for support but it always sides with the landowners. This year the police even refused to carry out an inquiry into who shot the rubber tappers who were camped out outside the IBDF offices on 27 May 1988. The gunmen were recognised and are well known round here and witnesses have made statements to the police, but they haven't done a thing.

In the case of Ivair's death,[5] it is obvious who hired the assassins. We don't know who the killers were but we know who paid them.

The mother of one of the injured boys with Chico Mendes in the union office on 28 May 1988.

Now, if you know who is behind a crime, you can easily get hold of the people responsible for carrying it out. The person who hired the killers was Cícero Tenório Cavalcanti, a candidate of the PMDB party. This is common knowledge and people have made statements to the police to this effect, but no progress has been made on the case and Cícero Cavalcanti hasn't even had to make a statement to the police.

5

Working Together

We rubber tappers have to organise and mobilise ourselves, because there's no point waiting for the government to help us. The only thing we can count on is our own level of organisation. One day we hope to organise a major *empate* right across the Amazon region. The future of the CNS and the extractive reserves will depend on how much resistance we can put up and how well organised we are.

The main force behind the CNS is still the Xapuri union, but we are forming new leaders and nuclei of support all over the Amazon region.

The CNS meets every six months. The strategic centre of the movement, in terms of communication and information, is the Institute of Amazon Studies, where Mary Allegretti, Paulo Chiesa, Bia and other friends work. They take care of the CNS' national and international links. We also get technical advice from Mauro Almeida at Campinas University.

One of the ways to increase support for the CNS and broaden the level of participation is to get discussions going with groups of rubber tappers, mainly in the communities that are already organised. In Xapuri we have 30 union branches which form the CNS support base in the area.[1] The same level of organisation exists in Brasiléia and Assis Brasil. We aim to have discussions with these groups of workers, these grassroots leaders, to work out ways of dividing up responsibility for spreading the education work across the region, and get the resources necessary to do it. The CNS is still a bit precarious because activists lack time to get more fully involved. Another problem is the sheer physical distance between us all and the difficulties of communication.

The dilemma of violence

So far we have used non-violent forms of struggle, and that's how we aim to keep it. If some day we need to use violence, it will be because we have been forced to do so by the circumstances, by the system and the policies of the landowners.

The *empate*s are organised in the following way. When a community is threatened by deforestation it gets in touch with other communities in the area. They all get together in a mass meeting in the middle of the forest and organise teams of people to take the lead in confronting the workers cutting down the trees with their chainsaws and so on — all this in a peaceful but organised way. These teams try and convince the workers employed by the landowners to leave the area. The rubber tappers also dismantle the camps used by those workers to force them out. We are often attacked by the police because the landowners always apply to the courts for police protection. The judicial system has always done what the landowners wanted and sent in the police and there have been a lot of arrests.

One important point is that the whole community — men, women and children — takes part in the *empate*. The women stay at the front to prevent the police from shooting us. The police know if they open fire, they will kill women and children.

I remember on at least four occasions, we were arrested and forced to lie on the ground with them beating us. They threw our bodies, covered in blood, into a lorry but we all sang hymns. We got to the police station, perhaps more than a hundred people, but they didn't have enough room to keep us there and we had to stand up in the corridors. In the end they had to let us go free.[2]

At the same time as 100 or 200 colleagues are involved in the *empate*, standing in the way of the chainsaws and scythes, we aim to have a team whose job it is to get information about what is happening back to Xapuri where another group will make sure it travels all over Brazil and the rest of the world. This is something we have only recently started to organise.

The trouble is that the landowners are quite happy about using violence. I'm very worried at the moment because they have, in fact, killed a few people. We know they intend to start by picking off some of the workers and then go on to attack our leaders. This year they killed Ivair, who was just beginning to emerge as a leader. He had got involved with our movement through the Church and was just learning the ropes.

Taking out quality hardwoods for exports.

I don't want to see this happening. I don't want anybody getting killed. There's no point in me or any of my colleagues dying. I don't think that dead bodies solve anything and I know that if that's the way things go, this place will become an inferno. We are going to do our best to see it doesn't happen. But if it did become necessary, I'm sure there would be 100, 150, 200 workers who would be ready to fight and decide this thing once and for all. But that would mean a bloodbath here in Xapuri, repression, and a lot more besides.

We don't want that to happen. We want to resist in a non-violent way as we are doing at the moment. We managed to deal with the Alves family by getting warrants for their arrest issued. It's now up to the courts to do what they are supposed to do, and see the law is upheld. This has helped us by creating a certain amount of goodwill in the local community. These days, for example, a lot of people who didn't even get on with me at first come up and say they support me. Middle-class people tell us how brave we are in facing up to the gunmen. Those criminals haven't been arrested yet but they have suffered a political defeat, and everybody knows it.

For us, the important thing is to continue to make a political impact. We feel our resistance can produce results through pressure by the press and lobbying organisations, at both a national and an international level. Our evaluation is that we should not go for a confrontation.

In the case of Cachoeira though, there was a moment in a very agitated mass meeting, last May, when I found myself in a tight corner with this argument. It's a good job we can keep calm in that kind of situation, otherwise I don't know what would happen. In this particular case a lot of workers had had enough of picketing and were proposing more radical tactics. In fact, they wanted to organise armed struggle against the police and the gunmen. They wanted a confrontation, but I feared the worst and argued that the movement should continue to use non-violent tactics, at least for the time being. We tried to show what effect the use of violence would have on our political support. It was a very animated meeting, but a very democratic one and we had a good discussion. There were about 400 people there, and in the end about 85 voted in favour of armed struggle. The rest voted to continue using non-violent tactics.

Neil MacDonald/OXFAM

Xapuri Rural Workers' Union building.

The agro-extractive co-operative

The idea of a rubber tappers' co-operative was first tried out in the *Projeto Seringueiro*. In the traditional estate the rubber tappers are locked into a system of debt bondage. When the old system breaks down, as it mostly has in the Xapuri region, dependence upon the estate is replaced by dependence upon merchants who travel into the forest by boat or mule train buying up the rubber tapper's production at knock-down prices and supplying the manufactured goods which the rubber tapper's family depends on at vastly inflated prices. A mark-up of 500 per cent on staples such as sugar is common. The rubber tapper's physical isolation means there are few options to this system.

However, if rubber tappers who are neighbours could work together to jointly stock and market their rubber and brazil nuts, getting their produce to the nearest town themselves, it would be possible to sell at the official minimum price and buy goods in bulk at wholesale prices.

This would mean finding the initial capital to start up such a co-operative and to acquire the mules or boats needed for transport. In 1980-83 the *Projeto Seringueiro* began testing the idea in three locations in the forests around Xapuri. Oxfam provided the funds. The idea was shown to be feasible and proved that by marketing and purchasing in this way, and without altering production techniques or levels at all, the members of the groups could maintain their previous consumption patterns during the rubber tapping year (April to December) and at the end of the year receive a sizeable cash income. This served both to recapitalise the co-operative and to give each rubber tapper a cash dividend.

If the group could then increase production by, for example, planting extra rubber trees on each trail or by planting additional fruit or palm trees in the forest and marketing the fruit, it would be possible to create forest production systems that reward existing forest dwellers, preserve the forest ecosystem, offer income levels that compare favourably with any other group of small producers in Brazil and represent an alternative regional development strategy to the ecological catastrophe of colonisation and forest clearance schemes.

Although there are difficulties involved in such co-operatives, not least in the training of the rubber tappers to administer the projects themselves, this is the model the CNS is seeking to introduce in the extractive reserves.

Co-operatives can sell their rubber in bulk, ensuring better prices and easier transport. Bundles of rubber ready for the mule train.

A rubber tappers' co-operative

The co-operative is a CNS initiative. The idea followed on from the proposal to create extractive reserves. We had to work out ways of improving the economic situation of the rubber tappers. They are exploited so much they often end up leaving the land and going to try their luck in the towns. The government and the landowners leave the rubber tappers in total poverty, right there in the middle of the jungle, hoping they will give up and leave the area.

The CNS is fighting for better living conditions for the rubber tappers so they feel their future lies here in the forest. The co-operative is already proving a success. So far it has relied on its own resources but we've just heard it's going to receive five million cruzados (£5,400) to help it get organised. Christian Aid, an organisation of the British Council of Churches, decided to give us the grant. For them it's a small grant, but for us it's a lot of money. With it we'll be able to improve the transport system taking the latex from the rubber producing areas to the strategic collecting points. This project was the fruit of a visit I made to London, where I met the people at Christian Aid. A representative of theirs later visited us when we were in the middle of an *empate*. He was able to appreciate our situation and decided to suggest the approval of a small grant.

The co-operative has to address itself to the problems of the rubber tappers but must also bring benefits to small farmers if they want to join. We hope the co-operative's activities end up going far beyond Xapuri and spread to the whole of the Acre valley, the rest of the state of Acre and ultimately all over the Amazon region. We know it will take a long time, but we'll manage it.

Health in the balance

On the question of health, the union took an initiative in 1985. At that time we had a certain amount of confidence in the State Health Secretary. To a certain extent, he was committed to the workers' cause, especially the rubber tappers. He was called Zé Alberto.[3] He had a team of doctors who were all committed to the rubber tappers' struggle, particularly to our fight for better health conditions. During the course of a year and a half we managed to build six health centres and have health promoters[4] sympathetic to our cause working among us.

Unfortunately we couldn't continue with the work because, as with anybody sympathetic to the labour movement in this state, Zé Alberto and the whole team of doctors got the push. However, the work went on because the health promoters were committed people. Some of them worked three years without a contract, without earning a penny. But they carried on anyway and showed they knew what they were doing and some of them now have a job and earn a proper wage from the State Health Department.

Our most serious problem is the lack of drugs and equipment for the health centres. We have to work hard to get all this from the hospital, because the Xapuri municipal council tries to make sure our health centres don't get a single pill. So now we're trying to find other sources of support through the CNS to keep things going.

A death foretold

Our movement grew out of the needs of the rubber tappers. We made a lot of mistakes but we learned from them. You know, people have to look after themselves, they have to fight and be creative. That's how we built this movement. We realised we had to fight to protect our way of life.

On 21 July 1980 they killed Wilson Pinheiro. On 27 July our comrades in Brasiléia decided to take justice into their own hands. So they killed Nilo Sérgio, one of the people who organised Wilson's murder. But what happened then, when our comrades suffered the violence of the police, when they were tortured? The movement was weakened because the level of grassroots organisation was weak.

CONTAG has a lot to answer for because of its attitude towards trade union organisation. It played an important role in setting the union up, helping it get on its feet, but it didn't give any attention to grassroots organisation or to preparing new leaders and activists. The landowners spotted this weakness when they they met in June 1980 and concluded 'if we kill Wilson Pinheiro and Chico Mendes, that will be the end of the trade union movement in Acre.'

At that time, here in Xapuri, we began to discuss all this. Raimundo Barros, the other main CNS leader in Xapuri, and I worked and lived together. After Wilson Pinheiro was killed, I slept somewhere else for three months, and then I got together with Raimundo and said: 'Look, as from today, we'd better keep apart, let's work in separate areas and both try to bring on new leaders. We must separate now because some day our enemies will catch up with us and kill us both. But if we separate and they kill you, I will keep trying to build the movement and if they kill me, you keep doing the same.'

From then on, we were never together. every six months to a year, I visited Raimundo's area and he visited mine. Today things have got better, because now there's a whole group of colleagues in each of our areas who are committed to the struggle. So now I don't have to worry so much about leaving my area.

These leaders don't show their faces so often, but they are around when the movement needs them. I can tell you the names of some of them. For example, in Cachoeira there's Manoel Custodio, a good leader. There's Raimundo Monteiro, Luís Tagino and other young activists, taking their first steps as leaders. There's another young lad, João Teixeira, who's incredible. You wouldn't believe it to look at him, but when you get talking you can tell he's got grassroots support and a great fighting spirit.

These people are the fruit of our movement's advances. After each stage in the struggle, we evaluate the situation, we learn from our experiences. The struggle teaches us many things. every day we learn something, while at the same time knowing we could be on the receiving end of a bullet at any time.

Fiernando Gabeira/Rex Features

'Chico Mendes — they have killed our leader, but not our struggle' — banner at the funeral.

We're involved because of our ideals and we'll never turn back. Our roots are too deep for us to think of giving up the struggle. It is a question of honour, a matter of principle. None of us would betray our movement. We all worked together to build up that spirit, that love. They would have to kill us all to destroy our movement and I can't see them managing to do that. I don't get that cold feeling any more. I am no longer afraid of dying and I know they can't destroy us. If any of us got killed, the resistance would still go on and it might even be that much stronger.

6

The Future

The prospects for our struggle have got much better. All that we've achieved over the last 15 years is just a drop in the ocean. Though extractive reserves have now been established in some areas and others are under consideration, they aren't enough even for one per cent of the people who live in the Amazon forest. But we've taken the first steps and we're optimistic about the future.

Since 1975, the rubber tappers of Brasiléia and Xapuri have carried out 45 *empates*. These have led to about 400 arrests, 40 cases of torture and some of our comrades have been assassinated, but our resistance has saved more than 1,200,000 hectares of forest (five per cent of the UK). We've won 15 and lost 30 of the *empates* but it was worth it.

Another very significant development has been the setting up of the co-operative, which will solve some of the fundamental economic problems of the rubber tappers. And it's the rubber tappers themselves who run it!

Support from abroad has also been very important. Little by little, we're building the same level of support here in Brazil, and we think we've succeeded in getting our case across to the public. This has all helped us win the establishment of extractive reserves.

On 30 June 1988, the regional representative of the Ministry for Land Reform and Development (MIRAD) stamped her feet on the ground and said the Cachoeira rubber estate would never be expropriated. Just 30 days later an order for the compulsory purchase of Cachoeira was issued. Since then, another reserve has already been declared, in São Luís do Remanso. The reserve there covers 40,000 hectares (150 square miles) on the border of the municipalities of Rio Branco, the state capital, and Xapuri. Another area of about 40,000 hectares has been set aside in the municipality of Brasiléia. There are also proposals for reserves in Assis Brasil and at places in the states of Rôndonia, Amazonas and Amapá thanks to the campaign mounted there by the rubber tappers and the CNS. There is another area of 60,000 hectares at Matanã in the municipality of Sena Madureira, Acre, a place I don't know.

These victories are the fruit of the resistance movement, organised by the CNS, which has succeeded in spreading the word about our fight for the Amazon right across the world.

More than ever, the rubber tappers are ready to fight. The single biggest boost to our morale was the victory of the rubber tappers of Cachoeira. That victory had an enormous impact throughout the region. People knew the rubber tappers there were up against powerful landowners with bloody assassins at their disposal. Between 18 March and the middle of April, we had pickets of almost 400 people out there in the middle of the forest, every one of them determined not to let a single landowner near the place.

An arduous road

Despite the creation of the CNS and the increasing level of organisation of the rubber tappers throughout the Amazon region, we have a long and arduous road before us. After the defeat of the land reform proposals in the Constituent Assembly, we know we have a big fight on our hands.

We are up against the political power of the landowners. Their movement, the UDR, has enormous influence throughout the country and in Congress. It was they who defeated the land reform proposals.

Here in Xapuri, the UDR is beginning to make its presence felt. Since April 1988, when it formally set itself up in Acre, the number of hired gunmen in Xapuri has increased, as have the number of assassinations and attempted assassinations of workers. These gunmen are in effect the armed wing of the UDR and we are the targets. It's a very difficult situation and we're going to have to work fast to bring new leaders on and build the movement up in the rest of the Amazon so as to prevent too much attention being paid to Xapuri.

The other big challenge is to mobilise public opinion, so that together we can force the government to expropriate more land.

Something else that's worrying us is that the government has pencilled in extractive reserves in areas where the rubber tappers are not organised and where the CNS is not involved. We are

'They are stealing the green from our national flag' — poster.

worried about what exactly is going to happen in these areas. Only when the rubber tappers have got the reins in their hands do we feel happy.

We are demanding that the government put compulsory purchase orders on more areas. The areas we want expropriated are those with big concentrations of brazil nut and rubber trees, areas rich in good quality hardwoods, areas threatened with burning. These are areas where a lot of rubber tappers live and work. But we want to go much further than that. We believe it's no good creating a few isolated extractive reserves surrounded by grazing land. The government has to expropriate many more areas where rubber tappers live and where there are conflicts over land.

Our second main demand is to do with education, health and the economic problems that the rubber tappers face. We want proper education and health programmes in the reserves, and we want a better system for marketing our rubber. If this happens, it will stimulate production and at the same time encourage the rubber tappers to feel at one with the forest and fight to protect it that much more.

We want to find ways to defend our people from the violence of the landowners, but organising a system of self-defence for our people is still at an early stage, and we're not yet clear on how we can organise something along these lines.

What should we do? How far can we go? The whole question is under discussion. We think the Second National Congress of Rubber Tappers will go deeper into this question. Any self-defence scheme will have to take into consideration the situation we face, a situation that is going to get worse now the UDR is getting stronger. Our only aim in all this is to strengthen the rubber tappers' movement and defend the Amazon.

Epilogue

Chico Mendes was shot at 6.45pm on Thursday, 22 December 1988. He opened the kitchen door and stood at the top of the steps preparing to go down to the outhouse at the bottom of the garden for a shower before supper. According to the forensic experts who were brought in from São Paulo, he was hit by a single shot from a .20 gauge shotgun fired at a distance of 8.2 metres. Eighteen pellets hit his shoulder and forty-two his chest.

Rarely can a death have been so accurately foretold by the victim. On 28 October Chico had sent letters to the governor of Acre, to the secretary of public security of the state, to the local superintendent of the federal police and to the judge in Xapuri, warning that his death was being planned. He named the brothers Darli and Alvarino Alves da Silva as the ringleaders and listed twelve other people he claimed were involved, including local politicians. On 1 November he had sent a letter to the headquarters of the CUT in São Paulo advising that a network of thirty gunmen controlled by Darli and Alvarino existed in Xapuri and that they had threatened to kill him. On 29 November Chico had sent telegrams to the governor, the secretary of public security and to the head of the federal police in Brasília repeating the information on the threat to his life and giving details of a meeting at the Alves da Silva ranch in Xapuri, the Fazenda Paraná, when local ranchers had gone over the details of his planned murder. On 2 December Chico had gone to a local newspaper, the *Gazeta do Acre*, and claimed that the local superintendent of the federal police was in league with the Alves da Silva brothers. On 5 December Chico had sent telexes to Brasília to the head of the federal police, to the minister of justice and to President Sarney, again denouncing the Alves da Silva brothers' plot to kill him. On the same day, the director of the Acre state police granted an arms licence to Darci Alves Pereira, one of Darli Alves da Silva's many sons.

On 6 December another local newspaper, *O Rio Branco*, owned by the then president of the local branch of the UDR, published a cryptic note entitled 'Large Bomb' which simply said, 'Very soon a 200-megaton bomb will explode and the repercussions will be country-wide. Important people may get hurt by the end of the story. Wait and see because our source is trustworthy'. On the night of the 17 December a local doctor, a Bolivian with a practice in Acre, was playing cards in a Rio Branco club. He was told by one of his fellow gamblers, a local rubber estate owner and one of the people named in Chico's letter of 28 October, that Chico Mendes would be 'dead within five days'. The garrulous gambler went further, saying that at that very moment a pick-up truck was parked outside the club with the weapons ready to take to Xapuri. The truck belonged to the then mayor of Rio Branco, and the driver was one of the mayor's bodyguards. The doctor, his conscience troubled, related the story to a friend, who went to the bishop, who vainly sought the help of the same federal police superintendent whom Chico had accused two weeks earlier of being part of the plot.

Against the advice of all his friends, Chico returned to Xapuri for Christmas. He knew what he was doing and appeared to have chosen to meet his fate head-on. Despite the barrage of warnings he had given the authorities over the preceding weeks, nothing had happened other than the state government's decision to provide two bodyguards, and he appeared to believe that nothing would be done to protect him. To the local authorities, he was at best a troublemaker grown too big for his boots, at worst a dangerous radical who was hurting them both politically and in their pockets. To the federal authorities in Brasília, he would have been virtually unknown. On 21 December, back in Xapuri, he said to his sister and to a friend that he did not expect to see in the New Year.

If the local ranchers and politicians behind the murder had imagined that the death would go unnoticed, lost in the Christmas holiday period and in the rural violence statistics (another 101 rural workers were murdered in land or labour disputes in 1988), within 48 hours they had recognised their mistake. Chico's death was international news within hours, a situation that caused the Brazilian press to give it more attention than it would otherwise have been granted. On the Saturday afternoon, the bishop held a packed memorial service in the Rio Branco cathedral. Political and trade union leaders arrived from the south of the country, joining hundreds of rubber tappers for the funeral in Xapuri. The federal

Fiernando Gabeira/Rex Features

The funeral of Chico Mendes in Xapuri on Christmas Day, 1988.

police chief arrived from Brasília to take personal charge of the investigation, bringing in forensic experts from São Paulo.

On the way back from the funeral, driving past the entrance to the Alves da Silva ranch, Fazenda Paraná, actress Lucélia Santos, one of the main intermediaries between Chico and the *Partido Verde* in Rio de Janeiro, saw the family at their celebration barbecue on the ranch. By the time the police arrived, the men of the family had fled into the forest.

On 26 December Darci Alves Pereira, the 22-year-old son of Darli, came out of hiding and gave himself up. He confessed to the murder, claimed he was the sole author of the crime and claimed to have been defending his father's honour in the light of the family's humiliation over the Cachoeira incident. The forensic evidence suggested that he had been present in the hideout at the bottom of Chico's garden, and could even have fired the shot. However, the evidence also proved that at least two people had been present and on more than one occasion. The ambushers had left behind, among other things, a rain-cape, two cigarette packets, five empty sausage tins, a plastic comb, a sock, a mirror and two bottles. The search continued for Darli and Alvarino Alves da Silva as well as one of their ranch-hands, suspected hired gun Serginho (also known as Jardeir) Pereira. On 7 January 1989 Darli Alves da Silva gave himself up to the police. He proclaimed his innocence, protested about the 'witch-hunt' of his family and expressed disbelief at Darci's confession. Darci withdrew his confession, claiming it had been made under duress. The Xapuri judge, Adair Longhini, held committal proceedings in early February 1989 and, on the basis of the evidence, committed Darli and Darci for trial by jury. Because trial *in absentia* is forbidden under Brazilian criminal law, Alvarino Alves da Silva and Jardeir Pereira who had disappeared without trace, could not be committed for trial. There was insufficient evidence on which to try any of the other members of the network of gunmen based at the Fazenda Paraná, one of whom, Zezão, was killed in Xapuri before Darci gave himself up.

Who are the Alves da Silva, how did they come to Xapuri and what was their grudge against Chico Mendes?

At the trial of Darli and Darci in December 1990 evidence was presented of a dozen other murders committed by the family over a 30-year period leaving a trail of blood across a great swathe of Brazil. Grandfather Sebastião Alves da Silva, his sons, Darli, Alvarino, Dari and Isaac, and their respective sons, a family of boorish, illiterate land speculators and cattle ranchers, all appear to have inherited the same psychopathic trait — the belief that the simplest way to deal with an adversary or to respond to a slight is to kill.

The family fled from the south-eastern state of Minas Gerais in 1958, wanted for the murder of muleteer Manoel Alves Pinto and his fifteen-year-old son, killed in February of that year in the municipality of Pocrane in the middle Rio Doce valley. The family next turned up in the expanding agricultural frontier of western Paraná, the southern state where, in the 1950s and 1960s the native pine forests were giving way to agriculture through a mixture of planned colonisation and violent landgrabbing. By 1973 the Alves da Silva family was participating in this process with the ruthlessness that was becoming their trade mark. Between 1968 and 1973 at least five murders are attributed to the family in the municipality of Umuarana: Salvador Basquetti and Vicente Fernandes do Carmo, killed by Alvarino in February 1968; neighbouring farmer Ângelo Urizi, killed by gunmen on the orders of Darli in a dispute over land in February 1969; local trader Antonio Pereira da Silva, shot in the back by Isaac in May 1973; and Acir Urizi, son of Ângelo, shot on Darli's orders in June 1973 in the continuation of the land dispute. Acir's widow gave evidence at the trial in Xapuri, and the details of the process of intimidation leading up to the murder constitute another chronicle of a death foretold and a chilling resemblance to the death of Chico Mendes.

Guns for hire

Alvarino had already disappeared from Umuarana following a shoot-out with the police. When arrest warrants were issued against Darli for the Urizi murders, he too left Paraná and headed for Amazônia. By 1974 they had bought their first piece of land in Xapuri. This was a period when the Rio Branco to Brasiléia road was built and *seringalistas* were cutting their losses and selling out to would-be ranchers. Darli had sold his 250-hectare farm in Umuarana and with the proceeds was able to buy 2,100 hectares alongside the road, just down from the turn-off to the town of Xapuri. Here, the family created the Fazenda Paraná out of what had been until the very recent past virgin forest in the interior of a *seringal*. By 1978 they had cleared 800 of the 2,100 hectares and had acquired 680 head of cattle. By 1990 their holdings had expanded to 5,000 hectares and the herd to 6,000 cattle, making them middle-sized ranchers by local standards. In the process, the family had carved out a reputation for being unusually violent, even in the context of the generalised violence that Chico Mendes relates in this book. In the space of fifteen years or so, between the mid-1970s and the late 1980s, the Acre valley was transformed from forest to pasture by the construction of the road and the sale of rubber estates to ranchers. *Seringueiros* were dispossessed of the lands they occupied, either by being told to go, by being offered derisory compensation or by outright force, and the forest was cleared. The participation of the Alves da Silva family in this process was different from that of neighbouring ranchers only in the psychopathic character of their use of violence.

The key prosecution witness at the trial was a fifteen-year-old youth, Genésio Ferreira da Silva. Genésio's sister is married to one of Darli's other sons, Oloci Alves da Silva, and Genésio lived on the Fazenda Paraná from the age of six until the arrest of Darli. (Darli has a reputed 22 children by five wives. One wife remained in Umuarana when he fled in 1973. The other four were living on the Fazenda Paraná at the time of Chico Mendes' assassination. One of these, Francisca da Silva Oliveira, died a violent death the day after Darli surrendered to the police; a jugular severed by a kitchen knife. Although registered as suicide, there are suspicions that this was a case of *queima de arquivo* — literally, 'burning the files', the elimination of those who know too much.) In his evidence to the jury, Genésio spelt out, with details of other murders, the prevailing climate of terror at the Fazenda Paraná as the Alves da Silva family and the *Mineirinho* brothers (Jardeir, Oscar and Amadeu Pereira, ranch-hands and gunmen) thought nothing of killing for the most futile motives. Examples:

● Two Bolivians calling at the Fazenda Paraná for water were killed by Darci, Oloci and the *Mineirinho* brothers 'to see what they were carrying in their rucksacks'. (It was cocaine). The bodies were dumped in a ditch and later buried in paupers' graves despite their carrying papers. (The police clerk in Xapuri was controlled by Darli).

● A ranch-hand, asking Darli's permission to marry one of his daughters, was killed and mutilated by Darci, Oloci and the *Mineirinhos* on Darli's orders.

● A fifteen-year-old petty thief, Zeca, who sold stolen parasiticide to Darli, was subsequently hunted down and killed by Darli, who left the body by the roadside.

● A youth who argued with the *Mineirinhos* at the local dance hall after Jardeir had made advances to his girlfriend was subsequently found dead near the cemetery.

Genésio also confirmed that Darci, Oloci, the *Minheirinhos* and Darli's nephews, Gentil Alves da Silva, (son of Darli's brother Dari), had killed Ivair Higino de Almeida in June 1988 (see p.68). In the meantime, Darci and Oloci had been tried and convicted in June 1990 for the shootings at the IBDF offices in May 1988 (see p.63). Both were sentenced to twelve years imprisonment and Darci was thus already serving this sentence at the time of his trial for the murder of Chico Mendes.

In addition to the general hostility towards the leadership of the rubber tappers' movement that the Alves da Silva family shared with the majority of local landowners and conservative politicians, the family had two specific motives for wanting Chico Mendes out of the way.

Showdown at Cachoeira

Firstly there was the Cachoeira affair (see p35). Cachoeira was a test case for Chico and the CNS, in addition to Chico's emotional attachment to the *seringal* where he had grown up. The CNS, the Xapuri rural workers' union and Chico personally had invested great effort into organising the rubber tappers at Cachoeira. They were *autónomos*, that is to say the *seringal* was no longer controlled by an estate owner and Chico had been pressing for the government to expropriate the area and hand it over to the rubber tappers in the form of an extractive reserve. To further this, the rubber tappers had agreed among themselves that all the *colocaçoes* (see p.13 for an explanation of the term) had to remain in the hands of the community. Anyone wishing to leave the community was obliged to sell their *colocação* to another member of the community, not to an outsider. Despite this agreement, at the end of 1987 one of the rubber tappers from Cachoeira, José Britto, had sold his *colocação* to Darli Alves da Silva. In March 1988 Darli sent in his men to occupy and clear the land he had bought. On 18 March, Chico, the Xapuri rural workers' union and the 67 families living on the Cachoeira estate organised an *empate* to forestall Darli's occupation of the area he had bought from José Britto. One hundred and eighty rubber tappers stood up against Darli's clearing gang and Darli backed off. His pride was hurt, he ran the risk of losing his investment, and he swore revenge.

Following the Cachoeira and the Ecuador *empates*, and the May shootings, the government was forced to act. As Chico relates on p.81, at the end of July the government expropriated the Cachoiera estate, which was declared a form of extractive reserve. The Alves da Silva family had lost its investment, and the threats began in earnest.

Darli's second motive for wanting Chico Mendes dead springs from the first. In the middle of this violently escalating situation, an IEA lawyer from Paraná learnt of the arrest warrant issued against Darli in 1973 for the Urizi murder and arranged for the Paraná police to issue a *carta precatória*, a form of inter-state warrant to be presented to the federal police in Acre. This was issued on 26 October 1988. The following day, Chico Mendes visited the federal police superintendent in Rio Branco to inform him of the *carta precatória* and on leaving saw Darli drinking in a bar in front of the police headquarters. The federal police superintendent, alleging the force had not been officially informed, did nothing. This led Chico to begin the desperate process of forcing the authorities to act, described at the beginning of this epilogue. In the meantime, Darli, tipped off either by the police or relatives in Umuarana, visited the Xapuri courthouse and asked the clerk if the warrant had been received. When told that it had, Darli told the clerk that Chico Mendes could now expect what was coming to him.

In his evidence at the trial, Genésio related details of a meeting of local ranchers with the Alves da Silva family at the Fazenda Paraná to plan the murder of Chico Mendes. The evidence coincides with the details contained in Chico's telegrams of 29 November 1988. Among the participants were the owner of the *O Rio Branco* newspaper and local UDR president, the mayor of Rio Branco, the *seringalista* card-player who subsequently tipped off the Bolivian doctor, another UDR rancher and a federal deputy who unsuccessfully contested the November 1990 governorship elections in Acre. Although a police investigation into the involvement of these other conspirators was begun, the investigator was withdrawn from the case at the end of 1989 and none of the suspects was even interviewed.

Genésio recounted that prior to the murder he had witnessed an exchange between Darli and Darci where the father had accused the son of not having the courage to carry out the deed. He also recounted that at nine o'clock on the night of the murder, as he was lying on his bed, he heard Darci and Jardeir running in. They said to Darli, 'the man is dead'. When Darli asked who had fired the shot, Darci replied that he had. Darli then announced that he would have a cow slaughtered the next day for the celebration barbecue. This version was corroborated by other residents of the Fazenda Paraná during the police investigation in early 1989, although under threat from the family, these witnesses either retracted their stories or disappeared. One of the ranch-hands who disappeared admitted that a group of six people had been staking out Chico's house, two at a time, on Darli's instructions. This fits with the evidence found at the scene. Those involved were sons Darci and Oloci, two of the *Mineirinho* brothers Jardeir and Oscar Pereira, Zezão and the informant. Zezão was killed in December 1988 and the informant disappeared before he could be brought as a witness to the trial. Both may have been the victims of *queima de arquivo*.

Other victims of the phenomenon included the two bodyguards with Chico Mendes the night he was killed. They were killed in separate shootings in 1989 and 1990. José Britto who had sold his *colocação* at Cachoeira to Darli was shot dead in Xapuri in January 1990. He had received a revolver as part payment from Darli. This was subsequently proved to be one of the guns used by Darci and Oloci in the May 1988 shootings. Their trial was to take place in June 1990 and Britto's evidence would have been incriminating. The mayor's bodyguard who on the night of 17 December was waiting in the pick-up outside the Rio Branco's club with the weapons to take to Xapuri was also subsequently killed.

When the trial of Darli and Darci for the murder of Chico Mendes finally took place in December 1990 it proved something of an anti-climax. The defence team consisted of three local lawyers from

J R Ripper/Imagens da Terra

In the dock. Darli and Darci Alves da Silva at their trial, November 1990.

Acre and the neighbouring state of Rondônia. One of them is cited on seven occasions in *Brazil Nunca Mais*, the dossier prepared by the Archdiocese of São Paulo on torture during the 1960s and 1970s, as having been involved in torturing political prisoners. He had also defended members of the Medellín cartel in Rondônia. Two of the three had previously defended the *Mineirinho* brothers on murder charges in Rondônia. Although they denied the link, most observers identified the three with the UDR. Prior to the trial, the defence explained its strategy pleading innocence, characterising Darci's earlier confession as having been obtained under duress and character assassination of the prosecution witnesses. In a bizarre attempt to play to nationalist sentiment, one of the defence lawyers claimed they would base the defence on their proof that Chico Mendes had been murdered by the CIA on the instructions of North American environmental organisations.

License to kill
In the event, when asked by the judge how he pleaded, Darci confessed to the murder. He claimed he had acted alone and that

his father was not involved. The defence strategy then changed. The defence continued to argue Darli's innocence on the basis of of lack of proof of his direct involvement in the shooting and in any conspiracy to kill. In the case of Darci, the defence now put forward two lines of argument in mitigation: an archaic concept of *inexegibilidade de outra conduta*, meaning that the accused had no alternative but to commit the crime; and justifiable homicide, since Darci was defending 'relevant social values' and the 'integrity of his father'. The lawyers were arguing that the defence of the Alves da Silva property rights and their reputation among their peers (ie other ranchers) justified the murder. The prosecution denounced this for what it was: a licence to kill. Fifteen-year-old Genésio gave his evidence in an assured and convincing way and the seven-person jury decided unanimously that Darci was guilty of the murder of Chico Mendes and by a six-to-one vote that Darli conspired to murder. They were duly convicted of premeditated murder, by ambush and for perverse motives and sentenced by Judge Adair Longhini to 19 years imprisonment.

In the Brazilian legal system a verdict from a jury cannot be altered by appeal, except in cases where appeal judges consider that the verdict is at complete odds with the evidence presented. A sentence of 20 years or more is open to appeal against the sentence (not the verdict) and Judge Longhini's intention is therefore clear. By sentencing them to 19 years (the maximum sentence would be 30 years) he effectively preempted any appeal against the sentence.

Satisfactory as the verdicts and sentences were for Chico Mendes' family, the rubber tappers, and their friends and supporters in Brazil and abroad, the prevailing feeling was that justice had only been partially done. The feeling is widespread that there exists, behind the Alves da Silva family, a network of conspirators and that these have successfully avoided investigation. The Alves da Silva are essentially small fry, illiterate and of low intelligence, whose trajectory from fugitive outsiders to middling ranchers, propensity to violence and unusual domestic circumstances are well known locally. For the more intelligent and scheming brand of local landowners and politicians, anxious to rid themselves of the threat that rural leaders like Chico Mendes pose, but equally anxious not to be seen doing so, a family such as this is a godsend. If Darli and his relations ever needed a personal motive for carrying out the task that others wanted, they felt they had been given it during 1988 with the Cachoeira and the Umuarana affairs. One of the witnesses reported that during a meeting on the Fazenda Paraná, Darli had asked the owner of *O Rio Branco* if it was all right to kill Chico Mendes. The reply was that it was acceptable provided it was like the previous cases and did not make an impact. The local rancher and media king (who owns television and radio stations in addition to *O Rio Branco*) must have subsequently decided that it would make an impact, and published the cryptic note referred to previously.

One of the many uninvestigated aspects of the case is that of the *O Rio Branco* news team that was in Xapuri within 90 minutes of Chico's death. The team claimed to have learned of the murder in Rio Branco, jumped in the paper's pick-up and sped to Xapuri. Even on a good day, the 200-kilometre journey takes three hours. At night in the rainy season, over a poor dirt road the journey takes longer. A police investigator the same night took six hours to get to Xapuri. A military policeman, curious about their claim, felt the bonnet of the pick-up. It was barely warm. The next day, *O Rio Branco* hit the streets in the morning with a laid-out front page covering the case. It is clear that the whole coverage was planned beforehand, and that the journalists were already in Xapuri when Chico was killed. The lead reporter subsequently fled Acre, claiming tht his life was in danger as he knew too much.

When Darli gave himself up on 7 December 1989 he appeared genuinely to believe that he would not stand trial. He must have felt he had guarantees from his 'friends' in high places. When he did eventually stand trial, it was clear that he and the lawyers aimed to sacrifice Darci to get Darli off. Even when convicted and sentenced, Darli's posture appeared that of a man who knew that sooner or later the power and influence of the shadowy group who stood behind him would win out. (He must also live in the knowledge that should he open his mouth he will go the same way as his many victims).

Darli walks free

This patience bore fruit on 29 February 1992 when the local appeal court in Rio Branco annulled his conviction. The defence lawyers had appealed against the conviction on the grounds that the jury had been influenced. The appeal court consists of four judges, one presiding and three deciding. Although the guilty verdict was upheld in the case of Darci, the court voted two-to-one to annul the guilty verdict for Darli. The two judges who decided in favour of Darli used the only argument open to them: that the jury had come to a decision that was incompatible with the evidence. Prior to the appeal the principal prosecution lawyer, from São Paulo, had declared that it would be unthinkable for the court to come to this decision. Interestingly, one of his colleagues on the prosecution side, a local lawyer representing Chico's widow Ilzamar, had warned that in the local context things were not so straightforward, that maybe the evidence and logic would prove less important than local pressures and influence brought to bear on the judges. In the event he was proved right, and the firm conduct of the original trial by Xapuri Judge Longhini was put into context: an exception to the prevailing rules rather than a signal that the days of impunity were over for those that order the murder of rural leaders.

At the time of writing this story is not yet finished. The prosecution has announced its intention to appeal to the High Court of Justice in Brasília and even to appeal to the Supreme Court. On the other hand, the defence lawyers are seeking a *habeas corpus* to release Darli from preventive detention pending his trial for the 1973 Urizi murder. If they succeed, he will be freed, and the chances of him disappearing are high, as his brother Alvarino has successfully done since the day of the celebration barbecue two days after Chico Mendes' murder. In his eyes, and those of his 'friends' he will have vindicated his belief in the virtue of patience and letting the local 'system' work to a favourable conclusion.

In the meantime, what has been happening in Amazônia in the three and a half years since Chico Mendes gave the interview in this book? Has the situation of forest peoples changed over the period, and if so, for better or for worse? How has the Brazilian government reacted to the intense criticism of its environmental and human rights record?

Brazil has suffered international criticism from the press, governments and non-governmental environment and human rights groups on several issues over the period. In addition to pressure to bring the murderers of Chico Mendes to trial, these include concern over Amazon deforestation, pressure to halt the extermination of the Yanomami Indians, and outrage over the situation of street children, especially the widespread killing of children and youths by uncontrolled vigilante groups. However, Brazil also sought, and obtained, the privilege of hosting the 1992 UN Conference on Environment and Development.

The Sarney government was taken aback by the impact of Chico Mendes' murder. In an attempt to make genuine headway in resolving Brazil's environmental problems, or at least improve its external reputation, a major administrative reorganisation took place in early 1989. Previous federal agencies, including SEMAM (the special environment secretariat), IBDF (the forestry development institute) and SUDEPE (the fisheries development board) were fused into a new federal institute: IBAMA, the Brazilian Institute for the Environment and Renewable Natural Resources. The 1988 Federal Constitution, promulgated at the end of the year, represented at least on paper one of the more advanced statements of a nation's commitment to conserving its natural resource base. With the creation of IBAMA the government announced its environmental programme *'Nossa Natureza'* (Our Nature). Although criticised as insufficient, top-down and a public relations response to external criticism (some CNS leaders scathingly referred to the plan as *'A Natureza Deles'* — *Their* Nature), it did represent the first attempt by a Brazilian government to elaborate a national environment policy. IBAMA started life as a Frankenstein figure, a throwing together of different parts, too big in Brasília and understaffed in the field. Its president was former presidential press spokesman Fernando César Mesquita. The move did, however, send the right signals to other governments. The UK aid minister, Chris Patten, visited Brazil, went to the Amazon and signed the first bilateral environmental aid agreement. Other countries followed.

When he left office at the end of the Sarney government in March 1990, Mesquita complained that IBAMA had received nothing but promises. There was some truth in his complaint. After a year of negotiations with donor governments, IBAMA still did not have the additional funds necessary to create an effective forest protection service. The state of Pará, for example, almost the size of France, had only a few dozen IBAMA staff. During the burning season of 1989, IBAMA did not have access to any helicopters to monitor deforestation.

However, Mesquita did manage to perform one fundamental act on behalf of the rubber tappers. In January 1990 he arranged for President Sarney to issue a decree establishing the concept of the extractive reserve, in the terms that the CNS and Chico Mendes had been pressing for. The state would expropriate the area in question, compensating the *seringalista* or other former owners as necessary, a census and land-use survey would be conducted, the local community through its representative body would approve an environmental management plan for the reserve, and this would then form the basis of a long-term lease contract between the community and the state (represented by IBAMA). The reserve would be collectively administered and private property in land would not be admitted. Land transactions could only take place within the community; outsiders would not be able to obtain land within the reserve. The economic activities permitted would be those agreed in the management plan, and would be essentially non-predatory. This unexpected development was motivated both by Mesquita's genuine interest in the issue and by the Sarney government's desire to salvage something in public image terms from its otherwise dismal administration.

First extractive reserves

Simultaneously with this decree, Sarney signed a decree creating the first extractive reserve, 500,000 hectares (5,000 sq.km.) in the Upper Juruá valley, in western Acre. In March 1990, in the last days of the government, Mesquita persuaded Sarney to sign the decree creating a one million hectare reserve stretching from Brasiléia, through Xapuri, and into the municipality of Rio Branco. This huge reserve was to be called the *Reserva Extrativista Chico Mendes*. In addition, extractive reserves for rubber tappers were created in the states of Amapá and Rondônia.

In March 1990 the Collor government took office. Fernando Collor de Mello had narrowly beaten Lula, the PT candidate, in the second round run-off for the presidency in December 1989. Collor is a conservative maverick, whose playboy lifestyle appeared not to worry the *descamisados*, the shirtless poor, to whom his electoral strategy was addressed. The Collor de Mello family owns a media empire in the poor northeastern state of Alagoas, and Collor's use of television probably won him the election. Six months earlier, at the launch of his campaign, his rating in the polls had been three per cent.

Having no party base, in fact having run against the existing parties, Collor had a free hand in putting together his government. It was a mixture of unknowns and quixotic appointments, which involved a good deal of playing to the gallery. He appointed football star Zico as federal sports secretary, and to the newly created federal environment secretariat (SEMAM) he appointed the environmentalist José Lutzenberger.

The appointment, generally received by the environmental movement outside Brazil as a sign that real change could be expected, was received with much more reserve in Brazil. Lutzenberger had always been a lone operator, and his relations with grassroots movements and community organisations were often poor. In addition, he was known not to be interested in administration, negotiation and the operation of bureaucracies.

How then would he turn SEMAM and IBAMA (now subordinated to SEMAM) into effective structures? What would be his relative influence over government policies vis-a-vis, for example, the military or other ministries?

The ability of SEMAM and IBAMA to act over the two years of the Collor government has been limited by economic policy. The economic measures Collor announced on the day his government took office froze 80 per cent of the money in circulation and tried to control government spending. Environmental policy was hit particularly badly by budget reductions and Treasury reluctance to commit funds. There were particularly serious problems for SEMAM and IBAMA, which had external funding approved for environmental programmes but where the release of external funds depended on the approval of domestic counterpart funding. As a consequence, World Bank funds for the national environmental programme and for the national environment fund were not released as expected. The result has been an inability to effectively establish and protect those conservation units that exist: national parks, ecological reserves and environmental protection areas.

On the vexed question of Amazon deforestation rates, access to the satellite data continues to be difficult, and there have been disputes over their correct interpretation. However, there seems little doubt that annual forest loss declined over the period 1989-91. The difficulties of interpretation include determining the relationship between observed fires and the consequent forest area lost, and the correct identification of the pre-burning vegetation — whether the burning occurred in virgin forest, in already degraded forest or in natural savannah regions within the Amazon basin.

Figures given to members of the German delegation accompanying Chancellor Kohl on his visit to Brazil in late 1991 suggest that the average annual forest loss in the period 1978-88 was 21,000 sq km per annum. In 1989 this was reduced to 17,800 sq km and further reduced to 13,800 sq km in 1990. Figures for 1991 will only be available in mid-1992, but the Brazilian government predicts that the total for the year will have fallen to around 8,000 sq km. One of the main reasons for the reduction is almost certainly the abolition of tax incentives for ranching projects in the Amazon basin. The scheme, introduced by the military government in the late 1960s, was suspended by the Sarney government in 1989. An attempt to restore tax incentives was made by the incoming Collor government, but then abolished at the beginning of 1991 following domestic and foreign criticism.

Burning questions

There are real questions over Lutzenberger's ability to influence government policy on a wider level, beyond conservation issues. There is little evidence that SEMAM' views are sought, still less acted upon by those sectors of the government responsible for activities with major environmental implications — energy, transport, agriculture, mining, sanitation. In the Interministerial Environment Committee that prepares the Brazilian negotiating positions for the June 1992 Conference on Environment and Development, the SEMAM positions tend to be isolated and ignored. Whilst SEMAM argues that Brazil should advocate a policy of compensation to countries that forego future income from forest development in the name of forest protection, that Brazil should favour linking the forest protection question to the discussions on climate change, and that Brazil should favour the establishment of international legislation on forest protection, the official Brazilian negotiating position is frontally opposed to these arguments.

On the question of public participation in environmental policy the situation is not much more encouraging. At the 1990 G-7 Summit in Houston, Brazil was invited to prepare a comprehensive forest protection programme. The World Bank and the EC were assigned to help in drafting the Pilot Programme, as it became known, and the indication was that substantial bi- and multi-lateral assistance would be approved at the 1991 G-7 Summit in London. One of the key questions would be the effective participation in the design and execution of the programme of non-governmental and community organisations. Throughout the first year of work, despite the recommendations of the World Bank and the EC advisers, SEMAM and IBAMA displayed little interest in consulting with NGOS or organisations like the CNS. This led to a crisis in relations, partially improved after the London Summit, when some initial funding for the programme was approved. However, the group of one hundred Amazon NGOs and grassroots organisations now interested in participating in the programme learned in February 1992 that the inter-ministerial group designing the programme, which includes SEMAM and the foreign and economics ministries, had decided to exclude NGO representatives from the programme's main committee. The participation of NGO representatives in the running of the programme had been previously agreed and figured in the documentation submitted to the G-7 for approval.

An evaluation of the Collor government's environmental policy, and Lutzenberger's success in achieving progress, is difficult to make. Certainly, neither has fulfilled the expectations of those that hoped for significant change. On the other hand, the Yanomami park has been established, albeit belatedly, and IBAMA and the CNS are negotiating the management agreements for the extractive reserves that exist. Progressive environmental policy is good for public relations, but not the highest of priorities in the middle of a severe recession and with a government trying to survive a political and economic crisis, with corruption and mismanagement scandals constantly surfacing. By late 1991 Collor had decided that political survival in a hostile Congress without a majority was impossible and brought the right-wing PFL party into his government.

Locally in Amazônia things have probably got worse for Indians and rubber tappers over the last year. The November 1990 governorship elections brought to power in Amazonian states governors opposed to everything that grassroots groups (and Lutzenberger) stand for. In Roraima, the local elite would dearly like to find a way to undo the Yanomami Park decree. In Amazônas, Governor Gilberto Mestrinho has picked public arguments with Lutzenberger, environmentalism and the concept of natural resource protection in general. In Acre, the PT candidate, Jorge Vianna, was defeated in the second round run-off by the right-wing PDS candidate, representing the old class of *seringalistas* (though not the ranching interests of the UDR variety). Vianna's platform was based on intensifying the search for a regional development policy based on sustainable use of the forest. The rubber tappers' movement would have had an important role in this process, as would FUNTAC and IMAC (the state environment agency). In the event, the PDS government over the last year has managed to reverse the faltering positive steps that were taken over the period 1988-90. IMAC, which created a model for other state governments in 1990 by making ranchers wanting to clear forest for pasture prepare environmental impact reports and have them examined at a public hearing, has been run down, as have FUNTAC's experiences in forest management. At the same time, leaders of the CNS continue to live under the constant threat of assassination. Throughout the period since Chico Mendes' murder, leaders of the rubber tappers' movement have operated under a series of death threats. Among those threatened are Osmarino Amâncio Rodrigues, president of the Rural Workers' Union of Brasiléia; Júlio Barbosa de Aquino, president of the CNS; Raimundo de Barros; Gumercindo Rodrigues, agronomist and adviser to the CNS. In July 1991 Pedro

J R Ripper/Imagens da Terra

Rubber tappers' leader Osmarino Amâncio at the graveside of his predecessor.

Ramos de Souza, vice president of the CNS and coordinator in the state of Amapá, was beaten up by unknown assailants in the state capital, Macapá, apparently as a result of his opposition to a state government road being built across an extractive reserve without the mandatory environmental impact report and public hearing. In September 1991 an attempt was made on the life of Antonio Macedo, CNS coordinator in the Juruá valley. These threats will tend to increase with the successful appeal of Darli Alves da Silva. The spectre of impunity for those who murder to protect their interests and privileges has returned.

When Chico's wife Ilzamar told Chico and the bodyguards to stop playing dominoes on the kitchen table and get ready for supper, she was doing what 60 million TV viewers were doing that same moment around Brazil. At 6.30pm the fateful episode of *Vale Tudo* ('Anything Goes'), TV Globo's nightly soap opera, began. *Vale Tudo* had been running for eight months, six episodes a week, and was drawing to its climax. The entire country knew that the villain of the story was going to be assassinated in that night's episode and Ilzamar did not want to miss a moment. That night it was Chico who died, not the villain. The programmers had fooled the audience, she would only be killed two days later. The story of the *telenovela* was typical of those at the time — jealousy, intrigue and hidden identity, set in the gilded world of the Rio urban upper class. This was a world far removed from that of Ilzamar and the vast majority of her 60 million fellow viewers.

Green soaps

Paradoxically, the shot that hit Chico also hit the *telenovela*. The majority of Brazilian editors, newscasters, newspaper readers and television watchers simply did not know who Chico Mendes was, what he had been struggling for, or why it was important. In the immediate aftermath, there was a collective struggle to get up to date with the facts and to understand why the outside world was giving another, almost routine, rural murder such attention. The issues of environment, poverty and human rights had never received serious attention in the mainstream media. To an extent, this began to change. *Telenovelas* with rural themes, where the protagonists were poor or the underdogs, began to appear and achieve a mass audience. The TV Globo hegemony was threatened for a time by a rival network whose slogan for its greened *telenovelas* was 'we show the Brazil that Brazil doesn't know' and whose locations were spectacular rural settings: the Pantanal, the pampas and pine forests of southern Brazil, Amazônia.

We should not read too much into this (and lately there has been a reaction back to rich urban settings); *telenovelas* are probably no more than the bluntest of instruments for changing popular perceptions, but the phenomenon is interesting. A revaluing of rural culture, of 'traditional' ways of life, a questioning of middle-class urban lifestyles and consumption patterns as valid aspirations for the poor in a country Brazil's size and with its natural resource base are prerequisites for that elusive concept of the 1990s — 'sustainable development'. Perhaps a barely discernible sea-change of popular attitudes is occurring in Brazil, but it is difficult to tell. Will the role of hosting the UN Conference on Environment and Development serve as a massive environment and development educational experience for the general Brazilian public? Perhaps, perhaps not. But should future historians, looking back to the 1980s, perceive a subsequent change in attitudes in Brazil, leading to identifiable changes in the way the nation organised its political, economic and cultural affairs, they should be aware that this occurred in part because of local level activities carried out by unknown and unsung activists who refer to their efforts as *trabalho de formiga* — the labour

of ants. One of those ants became known and sung about — abroad
and then at home — because he came to symbolise the spirit of the
time and lost his life in the process.

Tony Gross
Rio de Janeiro
4 March 1992

Footnotes

Chapter 1

1. Luís Carlos Prestes was a junior army officer who led the 'lieutenants' revolt' of 1924. From 1924 to 1927 he commanded the revolutionaries' 'long march' of 14,000 miles through the Brazilian hinterland.

   In 1931 Prestes formally joined the Brazilian Communist Party, spending the next four years in the Soviet Union. He secretly returned to Brazil, was imprisoned from 1936 until 1945, when he was elected senator for Rio de Janeiro during the party's brief period of legality (1945-47). He continued to be the most influential figure in the party until the military coup in 1964, after which he went into exile in the Soviet Union. He returned to Brazil with the general amnesty in 1979 and subsequently left the Communist Party.

2. Wilson Pinheiro was President of the Rural Workers' Union of Brasiléia until 1980, when he was murdered. (See chapter 2)

3. The National Council of Rubber Tappers (*Conselho Nacional dos Seringueiros* — CNS) was founded following the First National Rubber Tappers' Congress in Brasília in October 1985.

Chapter 2

1. Mary Helena Allegretti is an anthropologist who in 1979 wrote a thesis on the traditional rubber estate in Acre. In 1980 she began with others the *Projeto Seringueiro* co-operative and literacy programme with rubber tappers in Xapuri. In 1984 she joined INESC (*Instituto de Estudos Socio-Economicos*), a human rights centre in Brasília, lobbying Congress and government on Amazon issues. In 1986 she founded IEA (*Instituto de Estudos Amazônicos*) in Curitiba which provides support to rubber tappers and conducts research on Amazon issues.

Chapter 3

1. As explained in chapter 1, inter-union co-ordination has been prohibited in Brazil since the 1930s. Control over trade union activity was a principal concern of the military government after 1964. With the prospect of a return to civilian rule and democratisation in the 1980s, the trade union movement began to press for greater freedom.

   The most important labour meeting since the 1964 coup took place in August 1981 when 5,000 delegates from all over Brazil met in the first CONCLAT (*Conferencia Nacional das Classes Trabalhadoras* — National Conference of the Working Classes). From the outset there were clear divisions between the *autenticos* (those sectors led by Luís Inácio da Silva (Lula) and comprising the PT, the progressive Church and Trotskyist groups, radically opposed to the existing subordinate relationship of the trade union movement to the state), and the *Unidade Sindical* (Union

Unity) group composed of sectors benefitting from the status quo, backed by the PCB, PCdoB and PMDB.

Both factions were given equal representation in the commission to establish the planned Trade Union Congress (*Central Unica dos Trabalhadores* — CUT) to be founded at the second CONCLAT the following year. *Unidade Sindical* forced a delay until 1983, when two separate CONCLAT meetings were held. At the first, the *autenticos* went ahead with the founding of the CUT. *Unidade Sindical* resolved to continue with a rival body, initially retaining the name CONCLAT but in 1986 changing to CGT (*Central Geral dos Trabalhadores*) in reference to the trade union body prior to the 1964 coup.

CONTAG, the Confederation of Rural Workers' Unions, was one of the prime forces behind the separation of *Unidade Sindical* from the CUT and the creation of the CGT. The Xapuri Rural Workers' Union is affiliated to the CUT and Chico Mendes was a member of the CUT national executive.

Chapter 4

1. SUDHEVEA is a government agency created during the Second World War to encourage rubber production in the Amazon. Until 1987 SUDHEVEA provided health, supply and other services to the rubber estates. These services have been withdrawn and SUDHEVEA, now under the control of the Industry and Commerce Ministry, has become almost exclusively a price fixing agency, controlling the marketing and export of rubber. Since the mid-1970s, the agency has been controlled by Acre's big rubber producers.

2. The reference is to the administration of Flaviano Melo governor of Acre from 1987 to 1990. Flaviano represented the old local elite who controlled the rubber industry, and whose dominance was being challenged by a new elite of ranchers, mostly newcomers to Acre. He was also made aware at the beginning of his administration that Acre, the poorest and least important state in the Brazilian federation, could expect little financial support from the federal government in Brasília.

   It therefore made good political and administrative sense to appear to respond sympathetically to many of the demands of the rubber tappers and their supporters. It would pay political dividends, appearing as an alliance of *Acreanos* (albeit of both exploiters and exploited) against newcomers. It was also attractive financially since, by subscribing to the principles of sustainable development demanded by grassroots organisations locally and being advocated internationally, the state government was able to become attractive to international organisations such as the World Bank and the International Tropical Timber Organisation who were willing to fund its development programmes.

   State government publicity began referring to the 'ecological government of Acre', and promised to concentrate on promoting the rational use of forests rather than ranching. Controversial new roads and colonisation schemes were shelved. However, serious problems arose.

Weak state governments have little capacity to withstand the political and economic superiority of the federal government; the power of the ranchers is increasing, as witnessed by the growth of the UDR in Acre; and above all, an opportunistic alliance between a decadent elite and its former subjects in the face of the challenge from a new elite has few long-term prospects. The PDS state government elected in 1990 makes no pretence of having any sympathy with rubber tappers or extractive reserves.

3. *Seringueiros* trade brazil nuts using old 30 litre paraffin cans as the measure.

4. FUNTAC was created by the Flaviano Melo government in the belief that Acre had a future in silviculture. A pilot forest management project was funded by the International Tropical Timber Organisation and work was undertaken on sustainable forestry and local timber use, including appropriate low-cost housing for Rio Branco's exploding urban population. FUNTAC worked with the CNS and rural workers' unions to design and supply forest schools and health posts. The Canadian government approved a CAN$ 10 million research and forest management project with FUNTAC and the CNS. However, the current PDS state government has little interest in proceeding with these initiatives.

5. Ivair Higino de Almeida, 26, member of the Xapuri Rural Workers' Union and prospective PT candidate for councillor in the November 1988 municipal elections, was assassinated in a roadside ambush outside Xapuri on 18 June 1988.

Chapter 5

1. The union branches referred to belong to the Xapuri Rural Workers' Union, which includes non rubber tappers. However in areas where the forest has not yet been cleared nearly all union members are rubber tappers, explaining why the union became the support base for the CNS in those areas.

2. This paragraph is quoted from an interview published in *Chico Mendes*, a pamphlet by the CNS, CUT and Xapuri Rural Workers' Union. It is included here as a graphic description of an *empate*.

3. Chico Mendes is referring here to José Alberto Lima, Health Minister in Governor Nabor's administration in Acre, (1983-6). While in post, he made important innovations in the public health programme.

4. Health promoters are members of the community chosen to receive primary health care training and to be responsible for health and nutrition education and first aid.

Glossary

ABI	*Associação Brasiléira de Imprensa* Brazilian Press Association
ARENA	*Aliança Renovadora Nacional* National Alliance for Renewal (government party 1965-79)
autenticos	Trade unionists advocating radical renewal of the movement
BBC	British Broadcasting Corporation
CEDI	*Centro Ecumênico de Documentação e Informação* Ecumenical Documentation and Information Centre (NGO, Rio de Janeiro and São Paulo)
CESE	*Coordenadoria Ecumênica de Serviços* Ecumenical Services Network (NGO, Salvador)
CGT	*Central Geral dos Trabalhadores* General Workers' Central (trade union congress aligned with PCB/PCdoB/PMDB)
CIA	Central Intelligence Agency (USA)
CIMI	*Conselho Indígena Missionário* Indigenous Missionary Council
CNS	*Conselho Nacional dos Seringueiros* National Rubber Tappers Council
CONCLAT	*Conferência Nacional das Classes Trabalhadoras* National Conference of the Working Classes
CONTAG	*Confederação Nacional dos Trabalhadores na Agricultura* National Confederation of Rural Workers
CPT	*Comissão Pastoral da Terra* Pastoral Land Commission
CUT	*Central Unica dos Trabalhadores* Workers' Central (trade union congress aligned with PT and progressive Church)

FETACRE   *Federação dos Trabalhadores na Agricultura do Estado do Acre*
Federation of Rural Workers of Acre

FUNAI   *Fundação Nacional do Indio*
National Indian Foundation (federal government)

FUNTAC   *Fundação de Tecnologia do Acre*
Acre Foundation for Technology (state government of Acre)

IBAMA   *Instituto Brasileiro do Meio Ambiente e dos Recursos Naturals Renováveis*
Brazilian Institute for the Environment and Renewable Natural Resources (federal government)

IBDF   *Instituto Brasileiro de Desenvolvimento Florestal*
Brazilian Forestry Development Institute (federal government)

IEA   *Instituto de Estudos Amazônicos*
Institute for Amazon Studies (NGO, Curitiba)

INESC   *Instituto de Estudos Sócio-Economicos*
Institute of Socio-Economic Studies (NGO, Braília)

MDB   *Movimento Democrático Brasileiro*
Brazilian Democratic Movement (opposition party 1965-79, became PMDB)

MIRAD   *Ministério de Reforma e do Desenvolvimento Agrario*
Ministry of Agrarian Reform and Development

NGO   Non-governmental organisation

PCB   *Partido Comunista Brasileiro*
Brazilian Communist Party (pro-Moscow)

PCdoB   *Partido Comunista do Brasil*
Communist Party of Brazil (pro-Albania)

PDS   *Partido Democrático Social*
Social Democratic Party (conservative)

PMDB   *Partido do Movimento Democrático Brasileiro*
Party of the Brazilian Democratic Movement (MDB post-1979)

PSB   *Partido Socialista Brasileiro*
Brazilian Socialist Party

PSDB	*Partido Social-Democrata Brasileiro* Brazilian Social Democrat Party (formed from left of PMDB 1988)
PT	*Partido dos Trabalhadores* Workers' Party
PV	*Partido Verde* Green Party
SEMAM	*Secretaria de Meio Ambiente, Presidência da República* Environment Secretary, Office of the President of the Republic (federal government)
seringal	rubber estate
seringalista	rubber estate owner
seringueiro	rubber tapper
SUDHEVEA	*Superintendéncia do Desenvolvimento da Borracha* Rubber Development Board (federal government)
UDR	*União Democrática Ruralista* Democratic Rural Union (landowners' organisation)
UNI	*União da Naçoes Indígenas* Union of Indigenous Nations (non-governmental)

Brazil in Brief

Population	Total 150,368,000 (1990)
	Annual Growth 2.2% (1981-90)
	Urban: 74.9% (1990)
Area	8,511,965 sq km (35 times the size of the United Kingdom)
Principal Cities (1980 census)	São Paulo 8.5m
	Rio de Janeiro 5.0m
	Belo Horizonte 1.8m
	Salvador 1.5m

People

Origins	European 54.8%; African 5.9%; Mixed 38.5%. Brazil's indigenous inhabitants (Indians) number around 200,000
Main language	Portuguese
Religion	Roman Catholic 89.1%; Protestant 6.6%

Social Indicators

Infant Mortality	63.2: per 1,000 live births (1985-90)
Life expectancy	64.9 (1985-90)
Illiteracy	18.9% (1990)
Piped water	85% urban (1985) 56% rural

The Economy

GDP	$326,195m (1990)
Trade	Exports (1990) $37,701m
	Imports (1990) $24,193m
Principal Exports (1989)	Manufactured goods 71%
	Soya beans & products 8.6%
	Iron Ore 6.3%
	Coffee beans 4.7%
Trading partners (1987)	Exports: USA 27%; European Community 26%; OPEC 8%; Japan 7%; Comecon 7%; Latin America 6%
	Imports: OPEC 23%; European Community 22%; USA 21%; Latin America 11%; Japan 6%; Canada 3%
Inflation	1585% (1990); 466% (1991)
Foreign Debt	$122bn (1991)

Sources: Economist Intelligence Unit; UN Commission on Latin America and the Caribbean (ECLAC), Brazilian Government; World Bank; Inter American Development Bank.

Chronology — Acre

1750 onwards	Forest product collectors begin to enter upper Amazon rivers on a seasonal basis
1860s/70s	Collectors begin penetrating upper Purus and Acre valleys
1878	First permanent rubber estate begun on Acre river
1880-1911	Rubber boom — Acre Fina considered best quality rubber for export. North-east rural workers fleeing drought migrate to become rubber tappers
1911-1940s	Period of stagnation in the rubber industry
1942-45	Rubber estates re-activated under US/ Brazilian agreement. New wave of rubber tappers brought from north-east Brazil
1945-late 60s	Rubber estates subsidised by federal government
1970s	With removal of subsidies, owners abandon the rubber estates or sell to cattle ranchers from other parts of Brazil
1974	Rural Workers' unions of Xapuri and Brasiléia founded
1980	Beginning of literacy and co-operative projects in Xapuri. Increasing conflicts with ranchers. *Empates* begin. Wilson Pinheiro assassinated
1985	First National Rubber Tappers' Congress held in Brasília
1986	Chico Mendes unsuccessfully runs as a PT candidate for the State Assembly
1987	Chico Mendes lobbies Governors' meeting of Inter-American Development Bank. Visits UK. Receives UN Global 500 prize.
1988:	
May	Two rubber tappers shot during *empate* at Ecuador rubber estate
June	Rubber tappers' leader Ivair Higino murdered in Xapuri
October	Brazilian government signs decrees creating first three extractive reserves. Repeated death

	threats issued against Chico Mendes and others
December 1989:	Chico Mendes murdered
March	Second Congress of National Council of Rubber Tappers and First National Meeting of the Alliance of Forest Peoples, Rio Branco
1990: Jan/March	Outgoing Sarney government regulates legal procedures for extractive reserves and creates two large reserves in Acre: Upper Juruá (500,000 hectares) and Chico Mendes (one million hectares between Brasiléia and Xapuri)
Nov/Dec	PT candidate loses to conservative PDS in state governorship election. PT platform includes support to extractive reserves and to self-managed sustainable forest extractive industries.
December	Trial by jury in Xapuri of Darli Alves da Silva and his son Darci Alves Pereira for the murder of Chico Mendes. Both convicted of premeditated murder by ambush and sentenced to nineteen years imprisonment.
1991: September	Assassination attempt on Antonio Macedo, CNS coordinator in the Juruá valley.
1992: February	Local appeal court in Rio Branco annuls conviction of Darli Alves da Silva.

Chronology — Brazil

822	Brazil declared independent from Portugal
1865-70	Alliance with Argentina and Uruguay in war against Paraguay. Paraguay defeated
1888	Abolition of slavery
1930	Getúlio Vargas comes to power
1937	Vargas establishes authoritarian state, the *Estado Nôvo*
1954	Military threaten coup; Vargas commits suicide
1964	Military overthrow President João Goulart with US assistance
1968	Military hardliners crack down on political dissidents, using censorship, repression and torture. Economic 'miracle' begins
1979	General Figueiredo takes over as president, promising to restore democracy. The two party system is abolished and six new parties formed, including the PT
1982	Debt crisis breaks, forcing Brazil to turn to the International Monetary Fund (IMF) for assistance
1983	The IMF imposed austerity programme leads to a 3.5 per cent drop in national output and food riots in São Paulo
1985	The military complete the transition to a civilian government, ending 21 years of military rule. The new President is José Sarney, previously leader of the military's political party
1986	Government launches Plan Cruzado, an economic stabilisation plan which succeeds in bringing short-term relief to the economic crisis. It lasts just long enough to ensure a landslide victory for the government party, the PMDB, in state and National Congress elections
1987	The National Congress starts drawing up a new constitution which is finally promulgated in October 1988

1988	Municipal elections in November bring the PT to power in São Paulo and other major cities
1989	Fernando Collor de Mello elected president
1989-92	Brazil strongly criticised for its record on environmental and human rights issues, notably Amazon deforestation, genocide of the Yanomami Indians and widespread killing of street children.
1992 March	President Fernando Collor de Mello sacks environment minister José Lutzenberger for his public attack on IBAMA, the federal environment agency. Lutzenberer has accused it of corruption and mismanagement of foreign funds.
June	UN Conference on Environment and Development, Rio de Janeiro

Further Reading

Sue Branford and Oriel Glock, *The Last Frontier: Fighting over Land in the Amazon* Zed Books, London 1985

Sue Branford and Bernado Kucinski *The Debt Squads: the US, the Banks and Latin America*, Zed Books, London 1988

Catherine Caulfield, *In the Rainforest* Heinemann, London 1985, also published in paperback by Pan Books

Adrian Cowell *The Decade of Destruction: the crusade to save the Amazon rainforest* Henry Holt, New York 1990

Gilberto Dimenstein *Brazil: War on Children* Latin America Bureau, London 1991

Judith Gradwohl and Russell Greenberg, *Saving the Tropical Forests*, Earthscan, London 1988

Independent Commission on International and Humanitarian Issues, *The Vanishing Forest: the Human Consequences of Deforestation*, Zed Books, London 1986

Richard Knowles, Craig Johnson and Marcus Colchester, *Rainforests: Land Use Options for Amazonia*, pupil book and teachers' resource pack, OUP & WWF-UK, Oxford 1989

Kenneth Maxwell 'The Mystery of Chico Mendes' *New York Review of Books*, 28 March 1991, pp39-48

Francois Nectoux and Nigel Dudley, *A Hardwood Story: An Investigation into the European Influence in Tropical Forest Loss* Friends of the Earth, London 1987

Andrew Revkin *The Burning Season: the murder of Chico Mendes and the fight for the Amazon rainforest* Houghton Mifflin, Boston 1990

Jackie Roddick et al, *The Dance of the Millions: Latin America and the Debt Crisis* Latin America Bureau, London 1988

David Treece *Bound in Misery and Iron: The Impact of the Grande Carajas Programme on the Indians of Brazil*, Survival International, London 1989

Films:
Chico — I want to live, 1988, 40 minutes, colour, Central TV for Channel 4 (Despatches), Distributor: Central Independent Television International, 35-38 Portman Square, London W1A 2HZ

Death in the Rainforest, 1988, 40 minutes, colour, BBC (Panorama), Distributor: BBC Enterprises, Woodlands, 80 Wood Lane, London W12 0TT

Music:
Milton Nascimento *Txai* CBS 1990

Organisations for Action and Information:

Catholic Fund for Overseas
Development (CAFOD)
Development and Environment
campaign
2 Romero Close
London SW9 9TY
Tel: 071 733 7900

Christian Aid
PO Box 100
London SE1 7RT
Tel: 071 620 4444

Friends of the Earth
Tropical Rainforest Campaign
26-28 Underwood Street
London N1 7JQ
Tel: 071 490 1555

Oxfam
Oxfam 2000
Campaigns Unit
274 Banbury Road
Oxford OX2 7DZ
Tel: 0865 311311

Survival International
310 Edgware Road
London W2 1DY
Tel: 071 723 5535

Trocaire
169 Booterstown Avenue
Blackrock
Co Dublin
Ireland
Tel: 0001 885 385

World Wide Fund for Nature
(WWF-UK)
Panda House
Weyside Park
Godalming
GU7 1XR
Tel: 0483 426 444

BOOKS FROM THE LATIN AMERICA BUREAU
NEW
Faces of Latin America
Duncan Green

Exploring the region from Argentina to Venezuela, **Faces of Latin America** describes the people and the processes which have shaped modern Latin America.

The book celebrates the vibrant culture of Latin America's peoples and looks at some of the key actors in the region's turbulent politics with chapters on the military, democracy, the guerrillas, indigenous peoples, the Church and the women's movement.

Faces of Latin America also traces the roots of the continent's most pressing issues — underdevelopment and poverty, the environmental crisis, and the fight for democracy.

'A wonderful introduction. Duncan Green has humanized our neighbours without sentimentalizing them. Clearly the work of an author who knows Latin America — and cares.'
Richard Fagen, Stanford University

ISBN 0 906156 59 9 (pbk) £8.99/ US$16.00
ISBN 0 906156 61 0 (hbk) £18.99

NEW
Brazil: War on Children
Gilberto Dimenstein
Introduction by Jan Rocha

In **Brazil: War on Children**, journalist Gilberto Dimenstein interweaves first hand reportage, interviews and statistics to paint a picture of life for the children. He discovers a world of pimps, muggers, prostitutes and petty criminals; homeless children who live in fear of sudden death at the hands of the off-duty police and other vigilantes who make up Brazil's death squads.

The author interviews the Church workers who risk becoming death squad targets by befriending the children and trying to bring them hope. He talks to the authorities who turn a blind eye, to the killers and to the children themselves.

'It should be the duty of everyone who cares about children in any respect to read this book.'
Brian Milne, *International Children's Rights Monitor*

ISBN 0 906156 62 9 (pbk) £4.99/ US$10.00
ISBN 0 906156 63 7 (hbk) £12.99